THE
WEDDING
WI$E
PLANNER

THE WEDDING WI$E PLANNER

❧❧❧❧❧

SUZANNE KRESSE

The Wedding Lady™

❧❧❧❧❧

BERKLEY BOOKS, NEW YORK

This book is an original publication of The Berkley Publishing Group.

THE WEDDING WI$E PLANNER

A Berkley Book / published by arrangement with
the author

PRINTING HISTORY
Berkley trade paperback edition / February 1998

The Putnam Berkley World Wide Web site address is
http://www.berkley.com

ISBN: 0-425-15615-X

BERKLEY®
Berkley Books are published by The Berkley Publishing Group, a member of Penguin Putnam Inc.,
200 Madison Avenue, New York, New York 10016.
BERKLEY and the ''B'' design
are trademarks belonging to Berkley Publishing Corporation.

PRINTED IN THE UNITED STATES OF AMERICA

10 9 8 7 6 5 4 3 2 1

TO POMPA

Guess what?

I made the Big Leagues!

Contents

Introduction   xi

SECTION ONE—ORGANIZE   1

CHOOSE THE KIND   3
Kinds of Weddings   4
Weddings of the Millinneum   6

CALCULATE THE COSTS   7
Our Wedding Outline   8
The Adjustable Budget Chart   10
Who Pays for What   11
Tips on Tipping and Contracts   12

CAST THE PARTY MEMBERS   13
The Bridal Party Guideline   **15**
Vendor Information   17
Our Attendants—Women   19
Our Attendants—Men   20
The Parents' Wedding Duties   21
Places, Times, Dates to Remember   23
Bridal Gown Buying Guideline   **25**
Vendor Information   27
Sample Gown Contract   29
Cost Comparisons   30–31
Groomswear Rental Guideline   **33**
Vendor Information   35
Sample Tuxedo Contract   37
Cost Comparisons   38
Our Groomsmen   39

COUNT THE NUMBERS   41
Guest Guideline   **43**
Strategic Information   45

The File Card System 47

Guest List for Our Getaway Wedding 49

Guest List for Our Weekend Wedding 50

Our Weekend Wedding Program 52

Invitation Guideline **53**

Vendor Information 55

Sample Invitation Order 57

Cost Comparisons 58

The Etiquette of Addressing 59

Invitation Assembly—Easy to Follow 60

Announcement List 61

Registry Guideline **63**

Vendor Information 65

Sample Gift Registry 67

SECTION TWO—CONTRACT 69

SECURE THE ESSENTIALS 71

Engagement Guideline **73**

Vendor Information 75

Sample Jeweler's Appraisal 77

Cost Comparisons 78

The Marriage Laws 79

The Marriage License 81

Engagement/Wedding Newspaper Announcement 82

Ceremony Guideline **83**

Vendor Information 85

Ceremony Seating 87

Our Ceremony Program 88

Reception Guideline **91**

Vendor Information 93

Sample Booking Contract 95

Site Comparisons 97

Our Reception Worksheet 98

Miscellaneous Wedding Duties 99

Catering Guideline **101**

Vendor Information 103

Sample Catering Order 105

Cost Comparisons 106

Beverage Worksheet 107
Accessories and Favors 108
Balloon Decorations 109
Entertainment Guideline **111**
Vendor Information 113
Sample Contract 115
Cost Comparisons 117
Ceremony Music Schedule 119
Reception Music Options 121
Our Reception Outline 123
Reception Festivities 125
Photography Guideline **127**
Vendor Information 129
Sample Contract 131
Cost Comparisons 133
Video Guideline **135**
Vendor Information 137
Sample Videography Contract 139
Cost Comparisons 141

SECTION THREE—CELEBRATE 143

SELECT THE DISTINCTIVE **145**
Wedding Cake Guideline **147**
Vendor Information 149
Sample Order 151
Cost Comparisons 152
Flower Guideline **153**
Vendor Information 155
Sample Floral Order 157
Cost Comparisons 159
Our Floral Schedule 161
Pre-Wedding Party Guideline **163**
Facts and Information 165
Cost Comparisons—Bridal Luncheon Sites 166
My Bridal Luncheon Outline 167
The Bachelor Bash 169
Cost Comparisons—Rehearsal Dinner Sites 171
Our Rehearsal Dinner Program 172

Transportation Guideline   **173**

Vendor Information   175

Cost Comparisons—Luxury Vehicles   177

Honeymoon Guideline   **179**

Vendor Information   181

Cost Comparisons   183

Our Honeymoon Outline   185

Legal Guideline   **187**

Status and Address Changes   189

Sample Name Change Letter   191

VENDOR LIST AND RECORD OF DEPOSITS   **193**

Introduction

As a bride today, you are older, more educated and probably paying for most of your own wedding expenses. You are a comparison shopper who is more value conscious than ever before. You have to be, because of the variety of wedding options now offered. For example, there are now several ways to buy a bridal gown, and wedding gift registries now range from department stores to mortgage companies, and everything in between. Truly, these varieties have turned the nineties into a time for gathering and sifting wedding information. It is a decade when not only are time and money important, but intelligent buying decisions are also key.

Since 1987, I have presented my WeddingWI$E program to over one million brides at the largest bridal shows held in America's biggest wedding markets. I literally teach brides how to become wiser wedding shoppers. I tell them what's hot and what's not, and show them the newest products and services offered from the national bridal industry. Brides love my WeddingWI$E tips and call me daily to discuss their personal planning problems.

This increased appetite for wedding knowledge, as well as your demand for better money-saving answers, has brought me to the conclusion that available planners are not meeting the real needs of today's brides. None really detail the important facts that brides, like you, need to know for contracting with wedding vendors. Most brides have never even seen a booking contract, let alone signed one.

I have observed that every bride plans her wedding at her own pace, and with her own priorities. And there is no *one* pattern for planning. The *only* date that is always important is your wedding date, because everything *must* be ready by then. I believe that the key to that date's success is this Master Guideline that I have designed to enable brides, like you, to make the best buying decisions possible. Use it, and make your wedding planning . . . *wonderful!*

Section One

❦

ORGANIZE

CHOOSE THE KIND

I know that planning your wedding, the most important event of your life, is very exciting and you can easily get caught up in the whirl of it all. I also know that every bride wants to plan a spectacular event, which at first may seem a bit overwhelming. If you follow this book, which breaks up the giant occasion into specific categories, you can be assured that nothing will be forgotten and everything will be put in a simple order that you can easily handle.

As a bride of the nineties, you can plan any kind of wedding you desire. While most brides prefer a traditional one-day wedding event, a growing percentage of modern women want something different and more personal.

Getaway weddings, holiday weddings, ethnic and theme weddings—even a whole weekend wedding celebration—are new ways that allow these brides to express their flair for the unusual and elaborate.

Of most importance is that today, wedding etiquette can also be uniquely expressed. I have compiled a complete list of wedding celebration traditions that is included in this chapter. You may include these customs in your wedding in either a traditional or a contemporary way. Either way, you can be sure that your protocol will be perfectly proper.

KINDS OF WEDDINGS

THEME
WEDDINGS

Today, throughout the United States, more than 10 percent of the 2.5 million weddings are coordinated and celebrated with a theme. The bride, groom and their party dress in costumes suited to the theme. Invitations, decorations, transportation, the cake and musical entertainment are all coordinated into the theme. This kind of wedding is best suited for someone who enjoys research and wants to make her wedding a grand production. The local library, costume shops and local museums are all excellent sources for finding unique and authentic ideas in helping create your theme wedding.

SOME THEME WEDDING IDEAS

Medieval	Military	Fiesta
Circus	Sports	Cinderella
Victorian	Nautical	Tropical Isle
Roaring Twenties	Western	Rock 'n' Roll

GETAWAY
WEDDINGS

Want to get married on an exotic island or in a storybook kingdom? It's as easy as gathering twenty of your best friends and family and together flying away to an exotic island or a magic kingdom to experience a very exciting and different kind of wedding. In fact, resort hotels all over the world now offer special "Marriage Packages" which you can learn about through travel agents who specialize in honeymoon travel. The hotel's "director of romance" plans all the details for you, including flowers, music, a cake, photography and a video so you can relive every exciting moment. Best news—the cost of this Marriage Package is *one-third the price* of a hometown wedding for two hundred guests.

SOME POPULAR GETAWAY WEDDING LOCATIONS

Hawaii	U.S. Virgin Islands	Las Vegas	Poconos
Bahamas	Jamaica	Cruise Ships	Bermuda
Disneyworld	Puerto Rico		

Some people celebrate their marriage by including special ancestral traditions that tie their different heritages together. These emphasize the bond that a marriage creates and, at the same time, celebrate each culture's unique rites of passage. This kind of wedding, known as an ethnic wedding, combines distinctive foods, specialty entertainment and dances and time-honored traditional customs that are performed both during the ceremony and at the reception. Unique ethnic dress is featured as the wedding attire.

ETHNIC WEDDINGS

ETHNIC WEDDING SUGGESTIONS

African	Polish	Scottish	Greek
American Indian	Japanese	Mexican	Jewish
Ukrainian	Puerto Rican	Italian	Hawaiian

All year long, holidays brighten our lives and put us in a festive mood. Holiday music and decorations provide ready-made adornments that save wedding couples time and money. Holidays also allow the extra time off during which reunions of relatives and friends can be easily arranged.

HOLIDAY WEDDINGS

HOLIDAY WEDDING IDEAS

Valentine's Day	St. Patrick's Day	Fourth of July
Halloween	Christmas	New Year's Eve

A large number of weddings are now celebrated over a weekend. This provides both the leisure time to celebrate and also time for distant family and friends to visit and to catch up on one another's lives. This kind of celebration begins as early as Thursday, with a welcome home party. Friday can offer a variety of scheduled activities, adults can participate in team sports contests, go sight-seeing or just relax and visit. In the evening, all attend the rehearsal dinner party. Some couples hire a full-time babysitter for the weekend or set up a special ''kid's room'' where children can be entertained with games, swimming, tennis or other sports activities. Saturday is the wedding day. Sunday, late morning, a farewell brunch is planned, which can also include the opening of the gifts.

WEEKEND WEDDINGS

WEDDINGS OF THE MILLINNEUM
Different Ideas about Wedding Etiquette

Choose Traditional or Contemporary Methods. Both are correct and properly acceptable today.

TRADITIONAL	CONTEMPORARY
1. Man asks parents, then asks woman for her hand in marriage.	1. A woman can ask a man to marry.
2. Man surprises woman with ring and formally proposes.	2. Couples decide to marry and shop for rings together.
3. A diamond is the selected stone.	3. Rubies, emeralds, sapphires and other gemstones with diamonds are now used as engagement ring stones.
4. Parents of bride host engagement party. Father of bride announces news.	4. Couples hold engagement party to which parents, special relatives and all members of bridal party are invited.
5. Bride's family finances most of wedding expenses.	5. Couple pays wedding costs themselves. Parents contribute cash toward celebration.
6. Couple is formally married in a church or synogogue.	6. Clergy marries couples in hotels, private homes or a ''drive-thru'' window.
7. Father of bride escorts her down the aisle.	7. A bride is escorted by her mother, brother, uncle, or she walks down the aisle herself.
8. All wedding portrait photographs taken after the ceremony.	8. Wedding photographs taken (separately if necessary) before the ceremony to save time.
9. Wedding gown is custom ordered through a bridal salon. Delivery is 12–14 weeks.	9. Wedding gown is purchased at a bridal warehouse and can be taken home the same day.
10. Children participate as members of bridal party.	10. Children are eliminated as wedding guests.
11. Receiving line follows ceremony in vestibule or lobby of chapel.	11. Receiving line is reserved for entrance at the reception site.
12. Wedding invitations are sent to first and second generations of family and friends.	12. Wedding invitations are sent to immediate family and close friends only—guest limit is 100.
13. Champagne is the official toasting drink.	13. Sparkling wines or nonalcoholic beverages are served.
14. Brides register for fine china and silver at large department stores.	14. Bride and groom register at discount stores, banks, hardware stores, liquor stores and travel agencies. Most registry is computerized to avoid duplication.
15. All gifts are acknowledged with a personal handwritten note.	15. Photo ''thank you'' pictures of bride and groom on front with a personal written note on back.

CALCULATE THE COSTS

The wedding budget is one of the most crucial elements of wedding planning. Your outline will begin by using the form on the following page, the framework upon which you will build your magnificient event.

The adjustable budget that follows will help you to stay on track with your costs and ensure that you will never overspend. It's easy to use and even allows you to see how your costs compare with national averages. The keep-track chart in this chapter will help you to have instant access to every money detail of your wedding, including who will be paying for what and how much that cost is estimated to be.

My best advice are the contract tips I have explained for you. Every item you buy or service you hire for your wedding will require a contract with a deposit to secure the purchase.

Refer to these contract tips throughout your entire wedding planning and you will avoid big wedding mistakes.

OUR WEDDING OUTLINE

1. Kind of wedding: (Circle One):	Formal	Semi-Formal	Informal
2. Dates:	Day of Week 1st Choice _____ 2nd Choice _____ 3rd Choice _____	Date _____ _____ _____	Year _____ _____ _____
3. Ceremony time: (Circle One):	Morning	Afternoon	Evening

4. Estimated number of guests: _____

5. Bridal gown style desired: _____

6. Groomswear style desired: _____

7. Number of women attendants: _____

      Names:

      _____

      _____

      _____

8. Number of men attendants: _____

      Names:

      _____

      _____

      _____

9. Color scheme: _____

10. Ceremony site(s) we like: _____

    _____

    _____

11. Reception site(s) we like: _____

    _____

    _____

12: Reception time: From _____ to _____

13. Meal will be: Sit-down dinner _____
                         Buffet dinner _____
                         Other _____

14. Music: _____
                         _____

15. Special customs and
    traditions I want included: _____
                         _____
                         _____
                         _____

What is the total amount we
want to spend? $_____

Decorations we want: _____
                         _____

THE ADJUSTABLE BUDGET CHART

1. Fill in the estimated total costs you want to budget for your celebration.
2. Use the national average costs listings to determine how much you should be spending on each facet of your wedding.
3. Use the percentages as your buying guideline. Example: If you spend 5 percent instead of 3 percent for your wedding cake, then you have to cut back 2 percent on another item. If you follow this method, you will maintain the fixed total budget you originally decided on. Use this chart and you will never overspend.

Our ESTIMATED TOTAL BUDGET is $_____

WEDDING FACET	% TO SPEND	NATIONAL AVERAGE SPENT	OUR BUDGETED AMOUNTS
Bridal Attire	5%	$ 750	
Wedding Rings	12%	$1,800	
Invitations	3%	$ 450	
Ceremony Fees	1%	$ 150	
Reception Costs	35%	$5,250	
(Food	(25%)		
Beverages)	(10%)		
Decorations	4%	$ 600	
Music/Entertainment	7%	$1,050	
Photography	7%	$1,050	
Videography	3%	$ 450	
Flowers	12%	$1,800	
Wedding Cake	2%	$ 300	
Pre-Wedding Parties	4%	$ 600	
Groom's Attire	1%	$ 150	
Limousines	2%	$ 300	
Attendants' Gifts	2%	$ 300	
TOTALS	100%	$15,000	

Please Note: This does not include the honeymoon. Average Honeymoon cost is $2,500 for a 7 day 6 night getaway.

WHO PAYS FOR WHAT

OUR WEDDING EXPENSES	WILL BE PAID BY	ESTIMATED COST
Invitations/Wedding Stationery		
Bride's Attire		
Bride's Rings		
Engagement Party		
Clergymember Fees		
Groom's Attire		
Limousine		
Attendants' Accommodations		
Bridesmaids' Luncheon		
Bachelor Party		
Rehearsal Dinner		
Reception Site Fee		
Rental Equipment		
Reception Catering		
Reception Refreshments		
Wedding Cake		
Music/Entertainment		
Ceremony		
Reception		
Decorations		
Photographer		
Videographer		
Florist		
Attendants' Gifts		
Marriage License		
Honeymoon Travel		
Wedding Gown Cleaning		

TIPS ON TIPPING AND CONTRACTS

TIPPING   While most gratuities are included in the fees, some are not. It is customary to tip certain individuals who help to make your wedding day a success. Follow this chart of tipping protocol.

Individual	Proper Amount	Who Pays Tip
Clergymember (priest, minister, rabbi)	Usually a donation $25–$250	Groom gives tip to best man, who pays after the ceremony
Public Officials (judge, justice of peace, city clerk)	A flat fee ($25); some judges cannot accept money	Groom gives fee to best man who pays after ceremony
Limousine driver	Usual fee is 15% of bill	Wedding host pays bill upon receipt
Waitstaff, bartenders	15% of total food/bar bill	Usually included on bill, host pays any balance after reception

CONTRACTS

1. *Read it carefully*. Take contract home with you to review alone, and note all small print.
2. Always write out *all details* on your contract. Be sure to include:
   Delivery dates, times and places
   List of *all* merchandise you are purchasing
   List of *all* services that will be provided for you
   List of *all* deposits and the payment schedule for any balance owed
   Any cancellation fees and the refund policy contractor uses
3. Make the smallest deposit possible and use a credit card.
   Federal consumer protection laws guard all payments made with a credit card. These laws give recourse to the credit card company if the products or service that you purchased are not what you ordered.
4. *Always! Always!* Bring your contracts with you on your wedding day. If there are any differences about your bar bill, catering bill, decorations, baker or entertainment, you have a ready reference in writing.

IMPORTANT
Your contract *must* be dated and signed by *both parties*
in order to be legally binding.

CAST THE PARTY MEMBERS

THE BRIDAL PARTY GUIDELINE

Your bridal party is very special. It is your personal selection of those people in your life whose presence at your wedding will make it the happiest day of your life. That is why who you choose and how you choose them is so important.

When considering people, ask yourself: Is this person important enough to me that their absence will make me feel that something is missing?

Remember also that the essence of a wedding is the uniting of two families—therefore, when choosing remember: Family is first, friends are second.

Notes about

THE BRIDAL PARTY MEMBERS

Bridal Party Guideline
VENDOR INFORMATION

WHEN TO MAKE ARRANGEMENTS

Ask your attendants after your engagement has been announced to all parents and your own children.

❧

WHERE TO FIND THE BEST

MAID/MATRON OF HONOR—bride's sister or closest friend (male or female)
BEST MAN—groom's best friend or closest relative (including his father)
BRIDESMAIDS—relatives or friends (pregnancy no longer disqualifies a woman)
GROOMSMEN/USHERS—relatives or friends
FLOWER GIRL—relative or friend (best age range is 4–8 years old)
RING BEARER/PAGES—may be boys or girls ages 4–10 years

❧

WHAT TO WATCH OUT FOR

- The *only* attendants that you *must* have in your party are your honor/witnesses.
- They must be 21 years old to legally sign your marriage certificate after your ceremony.
- Parents may also serve as witnesses.

❧

WHAT IT WILL COST

The wedding couple is responsible for the housing, meals and transportation for all out-of-town attendants during the entire wedding festivities.

A WEDDING CUSTOM OR TRADITION

In England, a bride gives her attendants a cutting of myrtle (symbolizing love) from her bouquet. According to custom, if the plant roots and blooms, they will marry soon.

A Wedding Wi$e Tip

Worried about having too many relatives and friends to choose from? Put all females names in a top hat and have groom randomly draw the total number you want. Proceed with putting all male names into the hat, and you draw the total number you want.

IMPORTANT
FACTS
TO KNOW

1. There is no limit to the number of attendants you can have in a wedding party.
2. It is customary to give all the attendants a thank-you gift. Jewelry and a framed color photograph of the wedding party are the most popular attendant gifts purchased today by brides across America.
3. Today a mother may walk her daughter down the aisle.
4. The most common argument between a bride and her maids is over the style and color of the dresses. Forcing one's closest friends to wear clothes they hate—but have to pay for—will bring nothing but trouble. *Best Advice:* The bride and *only* the honor attendant should shop together to select the three favorite styles. Then all of the bridesmaids should be gathered to try on and help to choose the best style for all. Use this method and you will make everyone feel involved.
5. If you feel that the physical appearance of a relative or friend would detract from your bridal party, arrange for him or her to perform another special task, such as ceremony reader or usher.
6. Remember: The essence of a wedding is the uniting of two families.

Bridal Party Guideline
OUR ATTENDANTS—Women

Our wedding color(s) will be _____

Maid/Matron of Honor: _____
Address: _____
City: _____ State: _____ Zip: _____
Phone: (____)-_____ Size Dress: _____ Shoe: _____ Hose: _____

Bridesmaid: _____
Address: _____
City: _____ State: _____ Zip: _____
Phone: (____)-_____ Size Dress: _____ Shoe: _____ Hose: _____

Bridesmaid: _____
Address: _____
City: _____ State: _____ Zip: _____
Phone: (____)-_____ Size Dress: _____ Shoe: _____ Hose: _____

Bridesmaid: _____
Address: _____
City: _____ State: _____ Zip: _____
Phone: (____)-_____ Size Dress: _____ Shoe: _____ Hose: _____

Bridesmaid: _____
Address: _____
City: _____ State: _____ Zip: _____
Phone: (____)-_____ Size Dress: _____ Shoe: _____ Hose: _____

Bridesmaid: _____
Address: _____
City: _____ State: _____ Zip: _____
Phone: (____)-_____ Size Dress: _____ Shoe: _____ Hose: _____

Bridesmaid: _____
Address: _____
City: _____ State: _____ Zip: _____
Phone: (____)-_____ Size Dress: _____ Shoe: _____ Hose: _____

Junior Bridesmaid: _____
Address: _____
City: _____ State: _____ Zip: _____
Phone: (____)-_____ Size Dress: _____ Shoe: _____ Hose: _____

Flower Girl: _____
Address: _____
City: _____ State: _____ Zip: _____
Phone: (____)-_____ Size Dress: _____ Shoe: _____ Hose: _____

Bridal Party Guideline
OUR ATTENDANTS—Men

Our wedding color(s) will be _____

Best Man: _____
Address: _____
City: _____ State: _____ Zip: _____
Phone: (_____)-_____ Shirt Size: _____ Shoe: _____ Hose: _____

Head Usher: _____
Address: _____
City: _____ State: _____ Zip: _____
Phone: (_____)-_____ Shirt Size: _____ Shoe: _____ Hose: _____

Groomsman: _____
Address: _____
City: _____ State: _____ Zip: _____
Phone: (_____)-_____ Shirt Size: _____ Shoe: _____ Hose: _____

Groomsman: _____
Address: _____
City: _____ State: _____ Zip: _____
Phone: (_____)-_____ Shirt Size: _____ Shoe: _____ Hose: _____

Groomsman: _____
Address: _____
City: _____ State: _____ Zip: _____
Phone: (_____)-_____ Shirt Size: _____ Shoe: _____ Hose: _____

Usher: _____
Address: _____
City: _____ State: _____ Zip: _____
Phone: (_____)-_____ Shirt Size: _____ Shoe: _____ Hose: _____

Usher: _____
Address: _____
City: _____ State: _____ Zip: _____
Phone: (_____)-_____ Shirt Size: _____ Shoe: _____ Hose: _____

Usher: _____
Address: _____
City: _____ State: _____ Zip: _____
Phone: (_____)-_____ Shirt Size: _____ Shoe: _____ Hose: _____

Ring Bearer: _____
Address: _____
City: _____ State: _____ Zip: _____
Phone: (_____)-_____ Shirt Size: _____ Shoe: _____ Hose: _____

Bridal Party Guideline
THE PARENTS' WEDDING DUTIES

Wedding Facets	Task	Duty of
Engagement	Host an engagement party. Officially announce engagement and/or wedding date.	Bride's parents or parent with whom bride lives.
Guest List	Supply the complete list of family and friends (include full address and phone number).	Mothers
Invitations and Newspaper Announcement	First person listed on wedding invitation as host of wedding celebration.	Bride's parent(s) or parent who pays for wedding
Wedding Rehearsal	Arrive on time to practice their part in wedding ceremony.	All parents
Rehearsal Dinner	Host the dinner party/Attend party	Groom's parent(s)/All parent(s)
Wedding Gift	Financial situation dictates the generosity of the gift. Any gift is correct.	All parent(s)
Ceremony Seating (divorced parents)	Seated in row #1. Seated in row #3.	Parent who raised and housed bride Other parent and new spouse or escort Same applies to groom's parents.
Ceremony	Read special poems or passages. Act as best man or matron of honor. Escort bride down the aisle.	Any parent
Receiving Line	Stand in receiving line. Greet guests as they enter. Introduce bride and groom to distant relatives and friends.	Mothers
Photographs	Picture-taking together or with the family groups.	Individual decision based on what works best.
Reception	Socialize at individual tables.	All parents
Wedding Dance	Join in wedding dance.	Parents dance with spouse or another family member or a friend.
Gift-Opening Party	Host party, usually held in a private home the day following the wedding.	Either parent

Remember: This is *your* wedding. Whether or not your parents are divorced, they should all be willing to cooperate to make your day enjoyable. Be sensitive to your parents' feelings, and tell them that their presence is very important to you, but remind them that this day is ultimately for you.

Bridal Party Guideline
PLACES, TIMES, DATES TO REMEMBER

This page may be removed, photocopied and distributed to all attendants and immediate family.

The Bride's Attendants

Make sure your wedding attire is ready, including shoes, lingerie, makeup and accessories. Have your hair styled and your nails done.

Final Fitting _____ Date/Time _____

Location _____

Rehearsal Date _____ Time _____

Location _____

Rehearsal Dinner Location _____

Ceremony Date _____ Arrival Time _____

Ceremony Location _____

Where to Dress _____

Reception Location _____ Arrival Time _____

Special Instructions _____

The Groom's Attendants

Ushers are at the entrance as instructed at the rehearsal. As guests enter, the usher inquiries whether they are friends of the bride or the groom and seats them accordingly. No guests are to be seated after the bride's mother has been seated.

Final Fitting _____ Date/Time _____

Location _____

Rehearsal Date _____ Time _____

Location _____

Rehearsal Dinner Location _____

Ceremony Date _____ Arrival Time _____

Ceremony Location _____

Where to Dress _____

Reception Location _____ Arrival Time _____

Special Instructions _____

BRIDAL GOWN BUYING GUIDELINE

To a bride, her wedding gown is the most important purchase of the entire wedding. Study the sample gown contract I have included in this chapter.

Be sure to comparison shop before you decide. Use the cost comparison sheets in this chapter to remember the details about your favorite selections of bridal attire. Keep your own personal notes on the notes page.

If they are not specified, don't be afraid to insist that details such as the store's exchange policy or the delivery date of your dress are clearly printed on your order.

Remember: Bridal salons are very competitive and will include extras like free alterations, free cleaning or free delivery if you purchase your gown there. Feel free to ask about any of these special perks!

Notes about
BRIDAL GOWN BUYING

Bridal Gown Guideline
VENDOR INFORMATION

WHEN TO MAKE ARRANGEMENTS

Begin to shop no sooner than one year and no later than nine months before the wedding day.

❧

WHERE TO FIND THE BEST

Most full service bridal salons stock approximately fifteen bridal styles for the season. They can easily order any designer gown from any manufacturer pictured in bridal magazines.

A bridal warehouse offers over one thousand gowns in stock, sizes 4 to 24. No special ordering is necessary.

❧

WHAT TO WATCH OUT FOR

- As a consumer, if you want a certain designer gown, you can check with a manufacturer directly to verify that a store is one of their authorized dealers.
- Don't be fooled into paying heftily for a "look-alike" gown that has been made by a "replica" manufacturer.

❧

WHAT IT WILL COST

The average cost of a wedding gown today is $750. A deposit of one-third the cost is required at ordering time. This does not include any accessories such as your shoes, headpiece, veil, jewelry or undergarments. You can save up to 40% when buying at a bridal warehouse.

A WEDDING CUSTOM OR TRADITION

Brides are encouraged to include something blue in their wedding attire. History tells that early Jewish brides considered blue the color of fidelity, purity and love and wore blue ribbons on their wedding day.

A Wedding Wi$e Tip

Bring a camera when you shop. Let someone snap photos of you in your favorite try-ons. You can study them at home—before you decide. It is also good to have a picture of your gown when shopping for your bridesmaids' dresses.

**IMPORTANT
FACTS
TO KNOW**

1. Bridal salons carry *samples only*—gowns are usually "special ordered" unless they will sell you the sample. *Comparison shop*.
2. More than 40% of American women wear a size 14. Bridal stores now carry plus size styles that offer "figure flattering" selections.
3. Be sure to dress properly when shopping—wear heel size and undergarments you are planning to wear on your wedding day.
4. Try on headpieces while wearing your gown.
5. Check antiques and resale stores for unique heirloom/vintage bridal gowns.
6. Protect yourself—pay for your wedding gown with a credit card.
7. *Before you buy*: Check store's exchange and refund policy. Expect extra charges for alterations and gown pressing.
   When you buy: Put *everything* in writing—especially the delivery date.
   After you buy: Keep *all* receipts

Bridal Gown Guideline
SAMPLE GOWN CONTRACT

Here are necessary points that should be written on your wedding gown contract.

117 Southland Street Royal Oaks, CA 310-555-WEDD	**THE FITTING ROOM** Bridal Boutique	Hours: Mon.–Fri. 9–9 Sat. 9–6 Sun. 12–5

SPECIAL ORDER

Manufacturer's Name _____

Style # _____

Sized Ordered _____

Measurements: _____

Bust _____

Waist _____

Hips _____

Color Ordered _____

Special Requests _____

_____

Alterations Fee _____

Gown Storage _____

Pressing Charge _____

All Exchange or Refund policies (on front or back side) _____

READ ALL POLICIES—If you do not agree with something,
put a line through it.
(This means that it will not apply in your gown agreement.)

DELIVERY DATE *This is a MUST!*
(If the gown is never delivered your refund should be 100%.)

TOTAL PRICE _____
DEPOSIT PAID _____
BALANCE DUE _____

PAYMENT SCHEDULE _____

_____

Buyer

For Seller
BE SURE they sign, too!

Bridal Gown Guideline
COST COMPARISONS—Bridal Gowns

LOCATION	1	2	3
Store Name			
Phone			
Contact Person			
Appointment Info: Date Time Address			
Hours Open			
Selection #1 Manufacturer Style # Price Rating (1–5)			
Selection #2 Manufacturer Style # Price Rating (1–5)			
Selection #3 Manufacturer Style # Price Rating (1–5)			
In-Store Seamstress Alteration Changes			
Accessories	Style/Price	Style/Price	Style/Price
Available in Bridal Store: Headpieces Slips Bras Shoes Garters Hosiery Veils Jewelry			
Deposit Required			
Delivery Time			

Bridal Gown Guideline
COST COMPARISONS—Bridesmaids Gowns

Shop with your honor attendant only. *Narrow your choices to the* best *three or four.*
Then, arrange a "one shop trip" with all the bridesmaids to try on and decide on your final choice.

LOCATION	1	2	3
Store Name			
Phone			
Contact Person			
Appointment Info: Date Time Address			
Hours Open			
Selection #1 Manufacturer Style # Price Rating (1–5)			
Selection #2 Manufacturer Style # Price Rating (1–5)			
Selection #3 Manufacturer Style # Price Rating (1–5)			
In-Store Seamstress Alteration Changes			
Accessories	**Style/Price**	**Style/Price**	**Style/Price**
Available in Bridal Store: Headpieces Slips Bras Shoes Garters Hosiery Veils Jewelry			
Deposit Required			
Delivery Time			

GROOMSWEAR RENTAL GUIDELINE

Groomsmen have never been more fashionable than in the nineties. Today, gray, white and black are the classic colors that can be mixed and matched in jackets, vests, ties and trousers to make a unique wedding fashion statement.

Major tuxedo companies stock a large variety of colors, styles and patterns. Because all are competitively priced, shop around before you decide, and look for the "extra services" that they are offering. Keep comparison notes on the cost comparison sheet in this chapter.

Above all, make sure your *pickup date* is clearly marked on your rental contract. Also strongly consider appointing someone as your "tux handler" as I describe on page 35. It will save your entire party of groomsmen a lot of time and trouble. If you follow these chapter tips, you can be assured that yours will be a very happy rental experience.

Notes about

GROOMSWEAR RENTAL

Groomswear Guideline
VENDOR INFORMATION

WHEN TO MAKE ARRANGEMENTS

Begin to shop no sooner than six months and no later than three months prior to the wedding day. If wedding date will be around prom (April–May) or holiday (Nov.–Dec.), order six months in advance.

❧

WHERE TO FIND THE BEST

Any tuxedo shop that has a wide variety of styles, colors and accessories *in stock* is a specialist.
Experienced salespeople help you to select perfect styles.
Some shops also have tailored suits and Western-style suits and accessories to rent.
Tuxedo shops feature private dressing rooms and alteration equipment and services.

❧

WHAT TO WATCH OUT FOR

• Don't choose tuxedos from a catalog. See and feel what you are renting.
• Avoid shops that don't stock their own tuxedos. (Out-of-town warehouses send wrong sizes/colors that are too late to correct.)
• *Never* have out-of-town groomsmen bring tuxedos with them, unless you want a rainbow of menswear at your wedding.

WHAT IT WILL COST

Prices vary across America, but the average rental cost ranges between $30 and $60.
An average tuxedo rental includes a jacket, vest or cummerbund, trousers, suspenders, shirt, studs, cufflinks and a tie.
Shoes can also be rented but cost extra.

❧

A WEDDING CUSTOM OR TRADITION

Today, many male fiancés get to know his future father-in-law by making a date with him for lunch, golf or a sports event.

A Wedding Wi$e Tip

Choose a designated "tux handler."
Two days before the wedding this person picks up the entire lot of groomswear and checks that each suit is the correct size and all accessories are included.
He takes them to one central location (groom's home) where everyone will meet. Many *rushed* groomsmen appreciate this convenience.

IMPORTANT
FACTS
TO KNOW

1. Take along a swatch of your bridemaids' dresses to coordinate color with menswear.
2. Put the fathers in traditional black if they don't feel comfortable in contemporary tuxedos.
3. Tux rental stores are *competitive*. Some offer a free groom's rental (when bridal party is a group of five or more men) and feature accessory discounts. Be sure to *shop around* before you decide.
4. If your groom is wearing a military uniform, the free tuxedo could go to your father.
5. Make sure out-of-town groomsmen arrive at least one day before the wedding for a final fitting.
6. Send "mail measurement" cards to each out-of-town attendant. They can be measured at any tailor shop or men's clothing store, then send the cards back to you. You take them to the tuxedo shop.
7. Protect yourself—pay for your tuxedo rentals with a credit card.
8. *When you rent:* Put *everything* in writing—especially the pickup date.

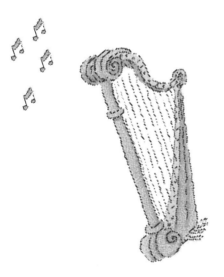

Groomswear Guideline
SAMPLE TUXEDO CONTRACT

Here are necessary points that should be written *on your tuxedo rental contract.*

35 Tulsa Lane • Canterbury, OH • 310-555-WEDD • OPEN 7 DAYS A WEEK

RENTAL AGREEMENT

STYLE #

COLOR

NUMBER NEEDED

ACCESSORIES INCLUDED

ADDITIONAL ACCESSORIES

PICKUP DATE—*A MUST!*

LATE RETURN FEES

All Exchange or Refund policies (on front or back side)

READ ALL POLICIES—If you do not agree with something, put a line through it.
(This means that it will not apply in your tuxedo agreement.)

TOTAL PRICE _____

DEPOSIT PAID _____

BALANCE DUE

PAYMENT SCHEDULE

Buyer   *For Seller*
                                BE SURE they sign, too!

Groomswear Guideline

COST COMPARISONS

LOCATION	1	2	3
Store Name			
Phone			
Contact Person			
Appointment Info: Date Time Address Hours Open			
Selection #1 Style Color Accessories Price Rating (1–5)			
Selection #2 Style Color Accessories Price Rating (1–5)			
Selection #3 Style Color Accessories Price Rating (1–5)			
Additional Accessories			
Deposit Required			
Late Fees			

Groomswear Guideline
OUR GROOMSMEN

This page may be removed and given to the tuxedo shop.

WEDDING OF _____ DATE _____

GROOM'S NAME _____ PHONE _____

IN-TOWN ATTENDANTS: _____

1. Name _____
   Phone _____ Relationship _____
2. Name _____
   Phone _____ Relationship _____
3. Name _____
   Phone _____ Relationship _____
4. Name _____
   Phone _____ Relationship _____
5. Name _____
   Phone _____ Relationship _____
6. Name _____
   Phone _____ Relationship _____
7. Name _____
   Phone _____ Relationship _____
8. Name _____
   Phone _____ Relationship _____
9. Name _____
   Phone _____ Relationship _____
10. Name _____
    Phone _____ Relationship _____

OUT-OF-TOWN ATTENDANTS: _____

We will need _____ mail measurement cards for the following attendants.

11. Name _____
    Phone _____ Relationship _____
12. Name _____
    Phone _____ Relationship _____
13. Name _____
    Phone _____ Relationship _____
14. Name _____
    Phone _____ Relationship _____
15. Name _____
    Phone _____ Relationship _____

COUNT THE NUMBERS

GUEST GUIDELINE

The first thing that a wedding couple needs to do after they set their date is not to book the reception site. That's right, how can you book a facility unless you know how many people your celebration will include?

Wedding couples and their parents need to gather and "guess-timate" how many people "have" to be invited. That total number should then be multiplied by $30 (today's national average cost of a wedding meal and one cocktail). If that total cost is more than you wish to spend, use the order of elimination list in this chapter.

Also be sure to copy the file card page and set up your own wedding file system. It's the surest way I can recommend to keep everything organized, and it's amazingly simple to do.

Notes about

THE GUESTS

Guest Guideline
STRATEGIC INFORMATION

WHEN TO MAKE ARRANGEMENTS

Compile your guest list immediately after you have chosen a specific wedding date. Both mothers should provide their family/friends lists, and you should compile a friends/business associates list. The sum of all three will be your official *count*.

WHAT TO WATCH OUT FOR

- Statistics show that one-fourth of the guests you invite to your wedding will *not* be able to attend.
- Be sure to include a response card in your invitation envelope. This is the *only* way to get an accurate count.

WHAT IT WILL COST

The national average cost to feed one guest and provide one beverage is $30. Multiply this number by your total number of guests and you will know approximately how much your reception bill will be.

A WEDDING CUSTOM OR TRADITION

In Scotland, guests carry on an old but cherished custom. They wash the wedding couples' feet, preparing them to set off on a new path.

A Wedding Wi$e Tip

The Card File System
(see page 47)
is the easiest way to
organize your guest list,
avoid duplication,
get an accurate guest count,
and simplify
your invitation ordering.

IMPORTANT
FACTS
TO KNOW

1. Each name on *all* lists should be followed by the complete address *and telephone number.* It is proper to call anyone who has not responded to your invitation by two weeks before the wedding date.
2. The only children who *have* to be invited to a wedding are the bride's and groom's immediate brothers and sisters.
3. Any person invited to your wedding ceremony should also be invited to your reception party.
4. If you have too many on your combined count, the following order of elimination should be used:
   1. First eliminate business associates,
   2. then parents of any attendants,
   3. then second cousins
   4. and finally remove family and friends who live more than two hours away.

Guest Guideline
THE FILE CARD SYSTEM

(This page may be removed and photocopied for as many cards as you will need.)

Attach each to a 3×5 file card and file alphabetically by last name. As you receive responses, mark the box in the <u>top right corner</u> $\boxed{R}$ for regrets, or $\boxed{A1}$ for acceptance, followed by the *total* number of attendees written on the response card.

Name _____ $\boxed{}$ Address _____ City _____ State ____ Zip _____ Name of Children _____ (under 18) at home _____ Phone (___) - _____ Thank-You Wedding Gift _____ Note ☐	Name _____ $\boxed{}$ Address _____ City _____ State ____ Zip _____ Name of Children _____ (under 18) at home _____ Phone (___) - _____ Thank-You Wedding Gift _____ Note ☐
Name _____ $\boxed{}$ Address _____ City _____ State ____ Zip _____ Name of Children _____ (under 18) at home _____ Phone (___) - _____ Thank-You Wedding Gift _____ Note ☐	Name _____ $\boxed{}$ Address _____ City _____ State ____ Zip _____ Name of Children _____ (under 18) at home _____ Phone (___) - _____ Thank-You Wedding Gift _____ Note ☐
Name _____ $\boxed{}$ Address _____ City _____ State ____ Zip _____ Name of Children _____ (under 18) at home _____ Phone (___) - _____ Thank-You Wedding Gift _____ Note ☐	Name _____ $\boxed{}$ Address _____ City _____ State ____ Zip _____ Name of Children _____ (under 18) at home _____ Phone (___) - _____ Thank-You Wedding Gift _____ Note ☐

Guest Guideline
GUEST LIST FOR OUR GETAWAY WEDDING

Name(s)	Party of: #

Guest Guideline
GUEST LIST FOR OUR WEEKEND WEDDING

Name(s)	Party of: #

Guest Guideline
GUEST LIST FOR OUR WEEKEND WEDDING

Name(s)	Party of: #

Guest Guideline
OUR WEEKEND WEDDING PROGRAM

Date _____ Time _____

Activity _____

Location _____

Dress _____

Comments _____

Date _____ Time _____

Afternoon Activity _____

Location _____

Dress _____

Comments _____

Date _____ Time _____

Evening Activity _____

Location _____

Dress _____

Comments _____

The Wedding Day _____ Time _____

Activity _____

Location _____

Dress _____

Comments _____

INVITATION GUIDELINE

Whether it's eloquently formal or country casual, your wedding invitation is the official notice of exactly what kind of wedding celebration your guests can expect.

By using the file card system, (see Guest Guideline), you can easily determine exactly how many invitations you will need to order. Shop around. Visit at least three different stationery or printing suppliers. Compare prices and designs.

After you have selected your favorite style and the typeface that completes your own special look, be sure to request a proof of your invitation. Check your printed proof for any typographic or spelling errors. Remember, once you initial this proof, you have released the printer of any liability. Therefore, you check it once, and have your groom check it twice—just to be doubly sure.

When you address your invitations, use the handy etiquette chart in this chapter. It has all the answers for proper addressing, including how children should be addressed. For those people whom you simply wish to send a written notice of your change of life status, follow the simple instructions on the announcement sheets also in this section.

Notes about

THE INVITATIONS

Invitation Guideline
VENDOR INFORMATION

WHEN TO MAKE ARRANGEMENTS

Wedding invitations usually are printed within two weeks from the date of order. Allow enough time to address and compile them to meet the traditional mailing date of six weeks before the wedding.

If your wedding will take place during a holiday, mail them eight weeks ahead of time.

WHERE TO FIND THE BEST

Invitations can be readily viewed at local stationers, or at many insta-print/copy-stores. You can save money by ordering directly from a mail-order manufacturer, found in most national bridal magazines.

Be sure to request a sample to see what you are buying.

WHAT TO WATCH OUT FOR

• *Please note*: The post office, now processing mail with computerized scanners, suggests that your return address be printed in the upper left hand corner of the *front* of the envelope. This will assure you of a speedy return if your guest no longer lives at that address.

WHAT IT WILL COST

Today, invitation prices vary greatly. Average cost is $25 to $100 per hundred ordered. Elaborate designs with real ribbons or lace attached, or those that ''pop up'' or play music, cost between $5 and $25 *each*. Expect to pay a 50% deposit the day you order.

A WEDDING CUSTOM OR TRADITION

Today, wedding programs that detail your marriage ceremony provide a treasured keepsake for all who attend.

Programs can also accommodate your guests with a map to your reception site printed on the back cover.

A Wedding Wi$e Tip

Computer calligraphy is now available in most cities.
Your invitation envelope can look ''hand lettered'' for 60% *less*.
Choose from more than 10 unique styles of type.

IMPORTANT
FACTS
TO KNOW

1. Simply count the total number of cards in your card file box. That is *all* the invitations you will need to order. You can add a few extras for mistakes and as keepsakes.
2. A standard wedding invitation, with all of its enclosures, can weigh 2 ounces and require 2 letter stamps. Take a complete envelope to the post office to check its exact weight. Consider a "LOVE" stamp.
3. Request an invitation proof from the stationer or printer. Check the type for any mistakes or spelling errors.
4. Include a simple printed map with your wedding invitation. It should detail directions to the ceremony as well as the reception site.
5. *Always* handwrite—*never* typewrite an address on your wedding invitation.
6. After they respond, send hotel/motel brochures to all out-of-town guests.

Invitation Guideline
SAMPLE INVITATION ORDER

The following are necessary points that should be written *on your invitation order.*

Announce It	
COMPLETE WEDDING ACCESSORIES	
110 West Midera Bay Drive 555-4004 Hours Mon.–Fri. 10–6	

SPECIAL ORDER	
QUANTITIES NEEDED	
Ceremony Invitations	
Reception Cards	
RSVP Cards	
Thank-You Notes	
Ceremony Programs	
INVITATION DETAILS	
Paper Stock	
Paper Color	
Ink Color	
Style of Type	
ACCESSORIES	
Candles	
Favors	
Napkins	
Guests Book	
Toasting Glasses	
Cake Knives	
Card Holder Rental	
Costs	
	TOTAL PRICE _____
	Deposit _____
	Balance Due _____
Payment Schedule	

PICKUP DATE–*A MUST!*
ALL Exchange or Refund Policies (on front or back side)
READ ALL POLICIES—If you do not agree with something, put a line through it
   (This means that it will not apply in your invitation agreement.)

_____   _____
Buyer   *For Seller*
                                                                BE SURE they sign, too!

Invitation Guideline
COST COMPARISONS

LOCATION	1	2	3
Store Name			
Phone			
Contact Person			
Appointment Info: Date Time Address Hours Open			

Selection #1
   Style
   Paper Color
   Ink Color
   Type Style
   Price
   Rating (1–5)			

Selection #2
   Style
   Paper Color
   Ink Color
   Type Style
   Price
   Rating (1–5)			

Selection #3
   Style
   Paper Color
   Ink Color
   Type Style
   Price
   Rating (1–5)			

Accessories			

Invitation Guideline
THE ETIQUETTE OF ADDRESSING

- Always write out names and words in *full*.
- The *only* abbreviations that should be used are "Mrs." "Mr." "Messrs." "Ms." "Dr." and "Jr."
- No symbols (e.g., &). The word "and" is written out.

GUEST	OUTER ENVELOPE	INNER ENVELOPE
Husband and wife	Mr. and Mrs. Paul Thomas	Paul and Sally Thomas
Wife kept maiden name	Mr. Paul Thomas and Ms. Sally Simpson	Paul and Sally
Wife uses hyphenated name	Mrs. Sally Simpson-Thomas	Paul and Sally

- Never write "and family." Children under age 18 should be listed on the inner envelope only.

Husband and wife and children under 18	Mr. and Mrs. Jerry Dole	Jerry and Susan Dole or Jerry and Susan
		Emily and Elizabeth

- Children over 18 should receive a separate invitation.

Two sisters over 18 at home	The Misses Nolan	Susan and Sandra Nolan
Two brothers over 18 at home	The Messrs. Brown	John and James Brown
Single woman	Miss Julie Jones	Julie
Single woman and guest	Miss Julie Jones	Julie and Guest
Engaged couple or couple living together	Mr. Jack Naples and Miss Debi Walters	Jack and Debi
Widow	Mrs. Mark (or Sylvia) Stevens	Sylvia
Clergymember	Reverend Joseph Adams	Father Joseph
Professor	Professor Walter Levy	Professor Walter Levy
Military Officer	Captain George Green	Captain George Green
Attorney	Attorney James Mathews	Attorney James Mathews
Doctor	Dr. Michael Calloway	Dr. Michael Calloway

Invitation Guideline
INVITATION ASSEMBLY—Easy to Follow

INVITATION AND ENCLOSURES

1. Place the response card in its envelope.
2. Place one stamp on each response card envelope.
3. Place the following closures into your invitation:
   - Response card in its stamped envelope
   - Reception card (if used)
   - Map (if used)
4. With all enclosures contained, insert invitation (open side up) into the inner envelope, with the front facing the back side of the envelope.

INNER ENVELOPE

- Handwrite the first and last names of all who are invited from that group. No children's names means no children invited.

OUTER ENVELOPE

- Insert the inner envelope with its front facing the back of the outer envelope.

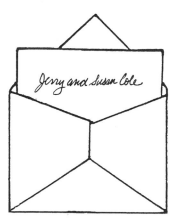

FRONT OF ENVELOPE

Invitation Guideline
ANNOUNCEMENT LIST

*Announcements are sent to anyone whom you did not invite to the wedding proper
but do want to notify. Announcements are sent the day after the wedding.*

Name: _____

Address: _____

City: _____ State: _____ Zip: _____

Name: _____

Address: _____

City: _____ State: _____ Zip: _____

Name: _____

Address: _____

City: _____ State: _____ Zip: _____

Name: _____

Address: _____

City: _____ State: _____ Zip: _____

Name: _____

Address: _____

City: _____ State: _____ Zip: _____

Name: _____

Address: _____

City: _____ State: _____ Zip: _____

Name: _____

Address: _____

City: _____ State: _____ Zip: _____

Name: _____

Address: _____

City: _____ State: _____ Zip: _____

Name: _____
Address: _____
City: _____ State: _____ Zip: _____

Name: _____
Address: _____
City: _____ State: _____ Zip: _____

Name: _____
Address: _____
City: _____ State: _____ Zip: _____

Name: _____
Address: _____
City: _____ State: _____ Zip: _____

Name: _____
Address: _____
City: _____ State: _____ Zip: _____

Name: _____
Address: _____
City: _____ State: _____ Zip: _____

Name: _____
Address: _____
City: _____ State: _____ Zip: _____

Name: _____
Address: _____
City: _____ State: _____ Zip: _____

Name: _____
Address: _____
City: _____ State: _____ Zip: _____

REGISTRY GUIDELINE

Registering your "wish list" of gifts is important because it enables your guests to learn exactly what you really want and need *and in the right colors!*

A wedding registry is a free service. Bridal couples are encouraged to register at several places, in order to allow guests a wide variety of prices and places to choose from. Brides are also advised to register immediately after they become engaged, so that people will have gift ideas for other wedding parties, such as the engagement party or the bridal shower.

Best Advice: Send *speedy* thank-you notes. If you use my thank-you note tips in this chapter, your guests will know not only that their gift was truly appreciated, but moreover, that it was received.

Notes about

THE REGISTRY

Registry Guideline
VENDOR INFORMATION

WHEN TO MAKE ARRANGEMENTS

After you have secured your wedding essentials, write out your "Wish List of Gifts."

Be specific—name the brands and sizes of all gifts you really love.

Register at several stores after you have your list completed.

Always choose name brand products, for quality and service assurance.

WHERE TO FIND THE BEST

Today registries are offered at department stores, discount stores, hardware stores, specialty boutiques, banks and travel agencies—to name a few.

Register at 2 or 3 stores (preferably those who offer a computerized system to give your guests a wide price range of gifts to buy).

WHAT TO WATCH OUT FOR

- Don't open any gifts at your reception party.
- Assign a trustworthy person to transport all gifts from the reception to your home.
- Inquire about a rider on your homeowner's or renter's insurance policy to cover loss or theft before the wedding or while you are honeymooning.

WHAT IT WILL COST

There is no cost to you to register at any store.

A WEDDING CUSTOM OR TRADITION

All wedding couples are obligated to write thank-you notes for gifts received. This courtesy *must* be finished no later than 30 days after the wedding date. The most cordial note includes a personal comment to the giver, names the gift and tells how you plan to use it.

A Wedding Wi$e Tip

Today, many registries offer "insert cards" that can be tucked into a shower invitation. It's a convenient way to inform all where they can find your "Most Wanted Wedding Gifts."

IMPORTANT FACTS TO KNOW

1. If a wedding is postponed, all gifts are kept.
2. If a wedding is cancelled, *all* gifts are returned with a simple note of explanation.
3. The best gift registries are computerized. Scanners allow you to shop at ease (no writing anything down). The computers cancel all gifts as they are purchased to avoid any duplicate purchases.
4. Be sure to know the stores return and exchange policies. Many stores today will not refund money unless you have the "gift receipt" with the product.
5. Some stores also provide gift wrapping and delivery of wedding gifts.
6. After the wedding, get a printout of gifts you wanted but did not receive. These items become ideal birthday, anniversary or Christmas gifts.

THANK-YOU NOTE TIPS

- Each shower and wedding gift should receive a thank-you note.
- All thank-you notes should be handwritten.
- All thank-you notes for money gifts should tell how you will use the money.
- Thank-you notes are signed by one person—the writer. But the message is from both (e.g., "Jim and I were delighted with the coffeemaker").
- If you receive a duplicate gift, or one you don't like, return it, but *do not* tell the giver.
- Sign your new name. Everyone will then know how to address you in the future.
- This note is *important*. It verifies that you did receive the gift. It will make the giver as happy as they made you with their thoughtfulness.

Registry Guideline
SAMPLE GIFT REGISTRY

Note: You locate all gift items with a scanner, which gives you the Sku #.

Russell's Gift Registry   Date: _____

Event: _____   **Event Date:** _____

Registrant: **Co-Registrant:**

Name (Last) _____   Name (Last) _____
Name (First, Initial) _____   Name (First, Initial) _____
Address _____   Address _____
City/State/Zip _____   City/State/Zip _____
Phone Day( ) ___ Evening( ) ___   Phone Day( ) ___ Evening( ) ___

Send gifts *before* event to: **Send gifts *after* event to:**
□ **Registrant** □ **Co-Registrant** *or* □ Other (below).   □ **Registrant** □ **Co-Registrant** *or* □ Other (below).

Name (Last) _____   Name (Last) _____
Name (First, Initial) _____   Name (First, Initial) _____
Address _____   Address _____
City/State/Zip _____   City/State/Zip _____

□ Yes, Gift Certificates are welcome.

Sku #	Qty	Item	Price	Sku #	Qty	Item	Price

Section Two

CONTRACT

SECURE THE ESSENTIALS

ENGAGEMENT GUIDELINE

You've been asked the big "M" question and you've said *"yes!"* Many of you may have already received or purchased your engagement ring. If you have, this chapter brings up three very important issues for you to consider. Read the facts about a written appraisal for your diamond, and be sure to have it evaluated by an independant appraiser.

You will also find here all the information you will need if you wish to formally announce your engagement in your local newspaper. Lastly, you will find a marriage license guideline in this chapter. It provides all of the specifics needed to secure this legal document.

If you are a couple who want to have custom-made matching wedding bands, or if you wish to purchase your fiancé's wedding ring, this chapter will greatly aide you in finding where to look, knowing what you can expect to spend and other information facts that will ensure that the quality of jewelry you are expecting is truly what you are buying. Again, be sure to shop around and compare prices. Make notes on the cost comparison page in this chapter.

Notes about

THE ENGAGEMENT

Engagement Guideline
VENDOR INFORMATION

THE ANNOUNCEMENT ORDER

- Tell both sets of parents.
- Inform any children involved.
- Tell supervisor and coworkers.
- Tell relatives and friends.

✤

WHERE TO FIND THE BEST

Reputable jewelry stores offer a fine selection of stones and settings.
Diamond wholesalers that sell to the public can also be found in the yellow pages.
Both offer a written appraisal of the rings you purchase.
You can write to the American Gem Society, 5901 West 3rd Street, Los Angeles, CA 90036 to receive a free consumer information kit and listing of reputable jewelers across America.

✤

WHAT TO WATCH OUT FOR

- You can take your ring to an independant appraiser to have it appraised seperately. If the appraisal is more than 10% different, return it to the original jeweler with complaint, or you can contact the Jewelers Vigiliance Committee at 1185 Avenue of the Americas, Suite 2020, New York, NY 10036 to investigate your contract.

WHAT IT WILL COST

The average cost of a half-carat diamond is between $500 and $1,000 A one-carat stone can cost between $2,000 and $3,000. Prices vary across the country.

✤

A WEDDING CUSTOM OR TRADITION

Swedish wives wear three wedding rings—one for the engagement, one for the marriage and one for motherhood.

A Wedding Wi$e Tip

Have a color picture taken of the two of you. Take it to a copy center and have copies printed on the back side of a postcard. On the front side, announce your wedding date and sign it with both names. This clever announcement gives plenty of planning time to all who will attend. It also allows them to see who the new family member will be.

IMPORTANT
FACTS
TO KNOW

1. Buy your ring from a professional jeweler who has been certified by the Gemological Institute of America.
2. Gemstones with diamonds are a unique, more economical look for engagement rings.
3. Men now favor wedding bands with diamonds.
4. Before you buy, check with the Better Business Bureau to see if there are any complaints filed against the jeweler.
5. Insure your rings *immediately* with a rider on your parents' or your own homeowner's/renter's insurance policy.

Engagement Guideline
SAMPLE JEWELER'S APPRAISAL

QUALITY JEWELERS, INC.
5 South Wabash Suite 1100
Chicago, Illinois 60603
(312) 555-1234

SAMPLE

TO WHOM IT MAY CONCERN:

This is to certify that we are engaged in the jewelry business, appraising diamonds, watches, jewelry and precious stones of all descriptions.
We herewith certify that we have this day carefully examined the following listed and described articles, the property of:

NAME _____

ADDRESS _____

We estimate the value as listed for insurance or other purposes at the current retail value, excluding Federal and other taxes. In making this Appraisal, we DO NOT agree to purchase or replace the articles.

DESCRIPTION	APPRAISED VALUE
One (1) 14k yellow gold lady's engagement ring set with a round diamond in the center weighing 1.16 cts., the color and clarity of the stone is SI1 "H" color. There are baguette diamonds on the sides with an approximate weight of 0.90 cts.	
VALUE FOR REPLACEMENT	$7,000

The foregoing Appraisal is made with the understanding that the Appraiser assumes no liability with respect to any action that may be taken on the basis of this Appraisal.

_____   _____
APPRAISER   DATE

Engagement Guideline
COST COMPARISONS

LOCATION:	1	2	3
Store Name			
Phone			
Jeweler			
Hours Open			
The Stone:			
Kind Size Shape (cut of stone) Color (grade D–I) Setting (14K–18K)			
White gold Yellow gold Platinum			
Side Stones			
Price			
Provide written appraisal			

Engagement Guideline
THE MARRIAGE LAWS

State	Age with parental consent Male	Female	Age without consent Male	Female	Maximum period between exam and license	Scope of medical exam	Waiting period Before license	After license
Alabama*..........	14a	14a	18	18	none	b	none	s
Alaska............	16z	16z	18	18	none	b	3 da.,w	none
Arizona...........	16z	16z	18	18	none	none	none	none
Arkansas..........	17c	16c	18	18	none	none	v	none
California........	aa	aa	18	18	30 da.,w	bb	none	h
Colorado	16z	16z	18	18	none	none	none	x
Connecticut	16z	16z	18	18	none	bb	4 da.,w	ttt
Delaware.........	18c	16c	18	18	none	none	none	c,s
Florida...........	16a,c	16a,c	18	18	none	b	3 da.	s
Georgia*..........	aa	aa	16	16	none	b	3 da.,g	s*
Hawaii	16d	16d	18	18	none	b	none	none
Idaho*............	16z	16z	18	18	none	bb	none	none
Illinois...........	16	16	18	18	30 da.	b,n	none	cc
Indiana	17c	17c	18	18	none	bb	72 hr.	t
Iowa*.............	18z	18z	18	18	none	none	3 da.,v	tt
Kansas*...........	18z	18z	18	18	none	none	3 da.,w	none
Kentucky.........	18c,z	18c,z	18	18	none	none	none	none
Louisiana.........	18z	18z	18	18	10 da.	b	72 hrs.,w	none
Maine	16z	16z	18	18	none	none	3 da.,v,w	h
Maryland.........	16c,f	16c,f	18	18	none	none	48 hrs.,w	ff
Massachusetts	16d	16	18	18	60 da.	bb	3 da.,v	none
Michigan	16c,d	16c	18	18	30 da.	b	3 da.,w	none
Minnesota........	16z	16z	18	18	none	none	5 da.,w	none
Mississippi........	aa	aa	17gg	15gg	30 da.	b	3 da.,w	none
Missouri..........	15d,18z	15d,18z	18	18	none	none	none	none
Montana*..........	16	16	18	18	none	b	none	ff
Nebraska	17	17	18	18	none	bb	none	none
Nevada...........	16z	16z	18	18	none	none	none	none
New Hampshire...	14j	13j	18	18	30 da.	b,l	3 da.,v	h
New Jersey........	16z,c	16z,c	18	18	30 da.	b	72 hrs.,w	s
New Mexico.......	16d	16d	18	18	30 da.	b	none	none
New York	14j	14j	18	18	none	nn	none	24 hrs.,w,l
North Carolina	16c,g	16c,g	18	18	none	m	v	none
North Dakota	16	16	18	18	none	none	none	t

(continued)

Ohio* 18c,z	16c,z	18	18	30 da.	b	5 da.	t,w
Oklahoma* 16c	16c	18	18	30 da.,w	b	none	s
Oregon...........17	17	18	18	none	none	3 da.,w	none
Pennsylvania*......16d	16d	18	18	30 da.	b	3 da.,w	t
Puerto Rico........18c,d,z	16c,d,z	21	21	none	b	none	none
Rhode Island* 18d	16d	18	18	none	bb	none	none
South Carolina* ...16c	14c	18	18	none	none	1 da.	none
South Dakota 16c	16c	18	18	none	none	none	tt
Tennessee 16d	16d	18	18	none	none	3 da.,cc	s
Texas*.............14j,k	14j,k	18	18	none	none	none	s
Utah...............14	14	18x	18x	30 da.	b	none	s
Vermont 16z	16z	18	18	30 da.	b	3 da.,w	none
Virginia............16a,c	16a,c	18	18	none	b	none	t
Washington 17d	17d	18	18	none	bbb	3 da.	t
West Virginia......18c	18c	18	18	none	b	3 da.,w	none
Wisconsin 16	16	18	18	none	b	5 da.,w	s
Wyoming..........16d	16d	18	18	none	bb	none	none
Dist. of Columbia* 16a	16a	18	18	30 da.,w	b	3 da.,w	none

*Indicates 1987 common-law marriage recognized; in many states, such marriages are only recognized if entered into many years before. (a) Parental consent not required if minor was previously married. (aa) No age limits. (b) Venereal diseases. (bb) Venereal diseases and Rubella (for female). In Colorado, Rubella for female under 45 and Rh type. (bbb) No medical exam required; however, applicants must have affidavit showing non-affliction of contageous venereal disease. (c) Younger parties may obtain license in case of pregnancy or birth of child. (cc) Unless parties are over 18 years of age. (d) Younger parties may obtain license in special circumstances. (e) Residents before expiration of 24-hour waiting period; non-residents formerly residents, before expiration of 96-hour waiting period; others 96 hours. (ee) License effective 1 day after issuance, unless court orders otherwise, valid for 60 days only. (f) If parties are under 16 years of age, proof of age and the consent of parents in person is required. If a parent is ill, an affidavit by the incapacitated parent and a physician's affidavit to that effect required. (ff) License valid for 180 days only. (g) Unless parties are 18 years of age or more, or female is pregnant, or applicants are the parents of a living child born out of wedlock. (gg) Notice to parents necessary if parties are under 21. (h) License valid for 90 days only. (j) Parental consent and/or permission of judge required. (k) Below age of consent parties need parental consent and permission of judge. (i) With each certificate issued to couples, a list of family planning agencies and services available to them is provided. (m) Mental incompetence, infectious tuberculosis, venereal diseases and Rubella (certain counties only). (n) Venereal diseases; test for sickle cell anemia given at request of examining physician. (nn) Tests for sickle cell anemia may be required for certain applicants. Marriage prohibited unless it is established that procreation is not possible. (p) If one or both parties are below the age for marriage without parental consent (3 day waiting period). (s) License valid for 30 days only. (t) License valid for 60 days only. (tt) License valid for 20 days only. (ttt) License is valid for 65 days. (v) Parties must file notice of intention to marry with local clerk. (w) waiting period may be avoided. (x) Authorizes counties to provide for premarital counseling as a requisite to issuance of license to persons under 19 and persons previously divorced. (y) Marriages by proxy are valid. (yy) Proxy marriages are valid under certain conditions. (z) Younger parties may marry with parental consent and/or permission of judge. In Connecticut, judicial approval. (zz) With consent of court.

From *The World Almanac & Book of Facts*, 1991 edition, copyright © Pharos Books 1990, New York, NY 10166.

Engagement Guideline
THE MARRIAGE LICENSE

The marriage license is a legal contract that binds the intent of two people to become husband and wife. License regulations may vary from state to state. *Please note*: This license does not mean you are married. In order for the license to be legal, it *must* be signed by a civil or religious official who is licensed in your state.

Documents WE will need	BRIDE		GROOM	
Identification (Driver's License)	Have	Must Get	Have	Must Get
Proof of Age (Birth Certificate)	Have	Must Get	Have	Must Get
Doctor's Certificate	Have	Must Get	Have	Must Get
AIDS or Other Blood Test	Have	Must Get	Have	Must Get
Citizenship Papers	Have	Must Get	Have	Must Get
Parental Consent (minors only)	Have	Must Get	Have	Must Get
Proof of Divorce or Annulment	Have	Must Get	Have	Must Get

County Clerk's Office _____

Address _____

Telephone _____

Hours _____

Appointment Needed _____

FACTS TO KNOW

- You should apply for your marriage license at least one month before your wedding date.
- Call the marriage license bureau (city clerk's office) in your city to get instructions.
- Both bride and groom *must* be present to get a license.
- When you go to the office, bring all necessary documents with you.
- The license fee ranges from $10 to $60.
- The license is *only* valid for a certain time frame (20 to 180 days). Allow enough time for your plans.

Engagement Guideline

ENGAGEMENT/WEDDING NEWSPAPER ANNOUNCEMENT

Here are guidelines for publicly announcing your marriage:

- List of all the newspaper names, addresses and phone numbers that you will send the announcement to.
- Call Fashion or Women's editor for lead time needed and average costs involved.
- Use form below as your information sheet. If you include a photo, an 8 × 10 or 5 × 7 black-and-white glossy professional photograph is needed.
- Print your name and full address clearly on the back of the photo if you want it returned.
- Make sure to insert cardboard for support and label the envelope **"PHOTO—PLEASE DO NOT BEND."**

Newspaper _____   Photo included _____

Return to:

Address _____   Name _____

Editor's Name _____   Address _____

Release Date _____   City_____ State_____ Zip_____

	BRIDE	**GROOM**
Full Name		
Parents' Names		
Address		
Parent's Name (if divorced)		
Address		
Schools Attended		
Special Clubs		
Military Service		
Employment		
Wedding Date		
Ceremony Site		

Officiant's Name _____

Description of Bridal Gown _____

_____

Honeymoon Destination _____

Residence after Wedding _____

(City)   (State)

CEREMONY GUIDELINE

One of the first arrangements that *must* be made is setting the date and time of your ceremony site. Because there are only 52 weeks in a calendar year, setting the date and time one year in advance is not too soon. Actually two years is not uncommon today.

Modern wedding ceremonies can be religious or secular. According to current marriage records, 85 percent of couples desire a religious service in a place of worship. However, this chapter will guide you about all ceremonies—what they require and what your costs will be.

This chapter will also aide you with the proper seating arrangements for a wedding ceremony, and provide you with a sample wedding ceremony program, should you choose to use one.

All of the specific facts that you will need to make your ceremony very special are included here.

Notes about

THE CEREMONY

Ceremony Guideline
VENDOR INFORMATION

WHEN TO MAKE ARRANGEMENTS

Because your ceremony and reception sites are your two most important arrangements, they are the first steps of wedding planning. Depending on the popularity of these sites, a two-year preregistration is not uncommon today.

RELIGIOUS CEREMONIES

- Held in a traditional place of worship.
- All aspects of a wedding ceremony, its costs and its other requirements, are guided by the rules or laws of each particular religion.
- Requires either a facility usage fee or, as a courtesy, a donation, usually given to the officiant who marries you.
- Usually requires prenuptial counseling and/or membership in that church
- Set up an appointment at your site of choice. Meet with the officiant. Ask every question you have and discuss details. Be sure to take a tour of the church proper to get on-site logistics.

WHAT TO WATCH OUT FOR

- Rules about photography and video taping during the ceremony
- Rules about musical selections and guest performers for your ceremony

WHAT IT WILL COST

Churches and synogogues can require a site fee or usage fee that ranges between $50 and $500. The officiant's fee can be a set amount or, it can be called a "contribution" (usually $50–$100). Sometimes there is an additional fee for the organist. Be sure to ask about these fees.

A WEDDING CUSTOM OR TRADITION

Consider including a "unity candle ceremony" during your service. This ceremony within the ceremony is performed at the altar. The bride and groom each hold one lighted taper and proceed to light one center candle together. This ceremony symbolizes the joining of the two families into one new family. You can also save that center candle and relight it as a special romantic memory during your first anniversary candlelit dinner.

IMPORTANT
FACTS
TO KNOW

Fill in the form below. It ensures that you have all of the correct information you will need as your wedding planning proceeds. You will find yourself referring to this information often as you meet with other wedding service providers, such as the photographer, florist and videographer.

Site _____

Address _____

City _____

State _____ Zip _____

Phone _____

Officiant _____

Ceremony Date _____

Ceremony Time _____

Rehearsal Date/Time _____

Music Rules _____
_____

Photo Rules _____
_____

Video Rules _____
_____

Dressing Room _____

Site Fee _____

Officiant Fee _____

Accessories and Fees _____

Candelabra _____

Candles _____

Arches _____

Flower Stands _____

Kneelers _____

Ceremony Guideline
CEREMONY SEATING

Reserve the first six pews on each side of the center aisle for special family members. You can also mark these pews with ribbons. Seat your family members according to the order below. If parents are divorced, use the right-side seating guideline. One pew between divorced parents gives breathing room to all.

The BRIDE'S Family and Friends (THE LEFT SIDE)	The GROOM'S Family and Friends (THE RIGHT SIDE)
Pew #1 Mother and Father	Pew #1 Mother and Husband/Companion
Pew #2 Sisters and Brothers	Pew #2 Sisters and Brothers
Pew #3 Sisters and Brothers	Pew #3 Father and Wife/Companion
Pew #4 Grandparents	Pew #4 Grandparents
Pew #5 Godparents	Pew #5 Godparents
Pew #6 Special Guests	Pew #6 Special Guests

Ceremony Guideline
OUR CEREMONY PROGRAM

Ask to see any samples of other ceremony programs at the printer/copy store you go to. Collect samples from your friends'/relatives' weddings

THE MARRIAGE CEREMONY OF

Bride _____

and

Groom _____
Date _____
Church Name _____
Street Address _____
City, State _____
Officiant's Name _____

PRELUDE (MUSIC/VOCALS)
1. _____
2. _____

SEATING OF PARENTS
1. _____

PROCESSIONAL
1. _____

THE BRIDE'S ENTRANCE
1. _____

READINGS (MUSIC/VOCAL)
1. _____
2. _____
3. _____

VOWS & EXCHANGE OF RINGS (MUSIC/VOCAL)
1. _____

LIGHTING OF CANDLES (MUSIC/VOCAL)
1. _____

COMMUNION (MUSIC/VOCAL)
1. _____
2. _____

RECESSIONAL (MUSIC/VOCAL)
1. _____

Parents

_____

_____

_____

_____

Grandparents

_____

_____

Organist/Musicians

_____

Soloist/Vocalists

_____

Maid of Honor _____   Best Man _____
Relationship _____   Relationship _____

Bridesmaid _____   Groomsman _____
Relationship _____   Relationship _____

Bridesmaid _____   Groomsman _____
Relationship _____   Relationship _____

Bridesmaid _____   Groomsman _____
Relationship _____   Relationship _____

Bridesmaid _____   Groomsman _____
Relationship _____   Relationship _____

Bridesmaid _____   Groomsman _____
Relationship _____   Relationship _____

Flower Girl _____
Relationship _____

Ring Bearer _____
Relationship _____

Pages _____
Relationship _____

On the back page of your program you can have a short personal message of thanks printed for your ceremony guests. You can also add any information about picture taking during your ceremony that your guests should be aware of.

RECEPTION GUIDELINE

Your reception site is your wedding *celebration* site. Do you want it to be a formal, upscale party or a festive picnic in the park? Today couples may choose any kind of site they want for their wedding party. The cost is the biggest consideration. This chapter gives you important facts about all the "charges" you could be expected to pay.

It is important that you do 3 things as you visit and evaluate different reception sites:

1. Compare sites and keep notes on the cost comparison page in this chapter.
2. Be sure to write down how much *each* of the *extra* charges is.
3. Protect yourself—reserve your site using a credit card (your wedding insurance card).

Above all, be sure that you read the contract *carefully* and be aware of what the *cancellation clause* requires. I've included a sample reception contract for you to review. Read over this typical contract and its terms. Ask the site manager for a copy of their contract. Take it home and review it carefully. If you have questions or disagree with any of the terms, discuss them with the manager and make adjustments—*in writing*—on the contract, so that you feel secure and pleased with the agreement.

Remember, too, that both you *and* the reception site manager should sign your agreement. This makes the terms of the agreement binding on *both* parties.

For all of your other miscellaneous reception details, use the handy wedding duties chart in this chapter. You will feel a real sense of accomplishment when these duties have been assigned to your family and friends. And don't be afraid to ask them—they are eager to help you!

Notes about

THE RECEPTION

Reception Guideline
VENDOR INFORMATION

WHEN TO MAKE ARRANGEMENTS

As soon as your guest list is compiled, start scouting for suitable reception accommodations.

Be flexible with your wedding date, as many popular reception sites can be reserved as far as two years in advance.

WHERE TO FIND THE BEST

More than 40% of America's wedding couples plan their reception at a hotel. The reasons: elegant atmosphere; customized menus; in-stock napkins, linens and centerpieces; uniformed waitstaff, convenient rooms for family and out-of-town guests at a discount and a free honeymoon suite for them.

WHAT TO WATCH OUT FOR

- Reception sites with one party room next to another (they hear you and you hear them).
- Check the cancellation policy. If you cancel, will you loose just your deposit, or will you be liable for a certain percent of your *total* reception costs? *Read your contract carefully!*

WHAT IT WILL COST

Some reception halls charge a flat fee ($50–$250) for the use of the room for a given number of hours. Catering can be brought in or offered seperately. The bar bill is also seperate.

Other reception sites require a deposit ($100–$1,000) which is applied toward your full bill, including all on-site catering and refreshments.

A WEDDING CUSTOM OR TRADITION

An old French custom is still practiced today as couples drink their reception toast from an engraved, two-handled cup called the *coupe de marriage*, which is usually passed on to future generations. Beautiful silver drinking cups that "fit" together are now available to purchase through catalogs or retail gift shops. And they can be engraved with your initials as a unique addition to your reception meal.

A Wedding Wi$e Tip

There are only 52 Saturdays in the year. That is why they are hard to secure and the most expensive. Save up to 40% by planning a Friday evening or Sunday brunch wedding reception.

IMPORTANT
FACTS
TO KNOW

1. *Don't sell yourself short! Look at a minimum of three reception sites.* Be sure to take notes and keep them on the comparison page in this chapter. It's the easiest way to see the whole picture concerning the differences in each facility.

2. Meet with the manager and take the time for a guided tour of the facility. Don't be afraid to ask questions as you walk around, and take notes.

3. Ask to see an itemized contract. Look for all of the *extra charges* such as setup, cake cutting, cleanup or any overtime fees.

4. Be sure to have *them* sign the contract, too. *Remember:* Two signatures are required to make any contract a legally binding document.

5. If possible, pay only a 10–15% deposit. Use your *credit card.* (It's your insurance for anything that is promised, but not delivered.)

6. Include on the bottom of the contract a written payment schedule for any balances due. Also write down the date that you *must* have your final count of guests. It is with this number that your entire food bill will be calculated. Even if ten guests do not show, you will still be responsible for paying for those ten meals.

7. Most couples who have held an outdoor reception or an "at home" wedding party confess that if they could redo it, they would *never* plan it that way. Why? Hidden costs such as tent lighting, air-conditioning, bug control and unpredictable weather. For at-home receptions the reasons were similar. Couples agreed that the costs for necessary items such as chairs, tables, dishes, linens, staff and decorations for the backyard and house proper were more than if they had held the event at a well-stocked restaurant party room or professional reception site.

Reception Guideline
SAMPLE BOOKING CONTRACT

LAKE VIEW COUNTRY CLUB

Date Booked ___May 20, 1996___

Date of Function(s) _SATURDAY, OCTOBER 25,_

Type of Function(s) _WEDDING RECEPTION_

___CKTLS-DINNER-DANCE___

Payment Information:

☒ Deposit required $ _500.00 NOW - $500.00_

☒ Payment at time of function   BY 4/25/97

☐ Payment in advance

☐ Direct bill

ORGANIZATION _____

Address _____

City _____ State _____ Zip _____

Coordinated by _____ Phone _____

Contact Person _____

APPROXIMATE AGENDA OF MEETINGS AND FUNCTIONS									
DATE	FUNCTION AND ANTICIPATED ATTENDANCE					TIMES		ROOM(S) RESERVED	RENTAL CHARGE
	BRKF.	LUNCH	HORS	DINNER	MEETING	STARTING	ENDING		
10/25/97				425		4:00 PM	CLOSE	JEFFERSON	

REMARKS	PLEASE NOTE THAT WE REQUIRE A $7000.00 MINIMUM OF HOSTED FOOD AND/OR
	BEVERAGE ON MASTER BILLING. IF MINIMUM IS NOT OBTAINED, THE CUSTOMER WILL
	BE BILLED FOR THE DIFFERENCE (CASH BARS, TAX AND GRATUITY ARE NOT APPLIED
	TOWARDS THE MINIMUM).

Approved this _____ day of _____, 19 _____   Lake View Country Club

Organization _____

By _____   By _____

                                                       Sales Representative   *Date*

PLEASE REVIEW BOTH SIDES OF THIS CONTRACT BEFORE SIGNING

WHITE: Sales Copy   YELLOW: Customer Copy   PINK: Office Copy

(continued)

For sit down meals of 100 people or more, you must limit your selection to one entree. (An additional charge of $1.00 per person will be applied if more than one entree is served to groups exceeding 100 people). Place cards with menu selections are required when choosing up to 3 entrees for groups less than 100 people. The cards are to be furnished by the customer.

Please note that taxes, gratuities and cash bar proceeds *are not* credited towards any hosted food and/or beverage minimums (when applicable).

The Club agrees to reserve the space necessary to accommodate the functions and requirements as listed. And, in consideration thereof, the customer agrees to use said space under terms and conditions to be agreed upon between the parties.

This contract is null and void if not signed by customer and returned along with any required deposit within 10 days after receipt. Accounts are due and payable in full at the completion of the function. All food and beverage is subject to 15% gratuity and applicable tax. All banquet checks are to be signed by the person in charge of the function. Any discrepancies must be identified at that time, otherwise the client must accept all incurred charges of the function. All groups are required to pay on one master bill.

The Lake View Country Club reserves the right to assign the facility most suited to the size and type of function being held. Specific room assignments can only be assured by adherence to the estimated attendance quoted at the time of booking.

This agreement may be cancelled by customer only in the event said function(s) is (are) cancelled and then only on notice in writing.

Cancellations will have 80% of their deposit refunded only if the Lake View Country Club is able to rebook another function at the required room minimum. Deposit will be refunded after the date of the function. If Lake View is unable to rebook the space and date, no refund will be granted.

Groups requesting tax exemption must submit tax number with a letter requesting such exemption at least 72 hours prior to the function.

Please note that the Country Club prohibits the serving of any food or beverage on our premises which is not purchased from the Country Club.

Two weeks prior to your banquet, please inform our Sales Office of your choice of entree, any specifics relating to your function, as well as your estimate of the number of guests.

Due to the fluctuating market conditions, prices are subject to change without notice. Firm food and beverage prices are quoted 30 days prior to the scheduled function, if requested. In arranging for private functions, the attendance must be definitely guaranteed and specified at least 72 hours in advance of the event. This specified number will be considered a guarantee, not subject to reduction, and charges will be made accordingly.

If you do not meet your guarantee, we do not allow you take the extra dinners, so please make sure your count is accurate.

The Lake View Country Club cannot be responsible for service to more than five (5) percent over the guarantee. If no guarantee is received by this office, the Club will consider the number of guests indicated on the copy of the Function Sheet and arrangements to be the guarantee and charges will be made accordingly.

If an open bar reception shall prevail, the customer purchases the drinks for the guests and is charged on a per drink basis only for liquor consumed. A 15% service charge shall be applied on an open bar.

Minors are not allowed to consume alcoholic beverages. You are responsible to assist us in policing minor guests in your party.

Functions will be staffed as required to properly service the event. Any additional or specific staffing will be charged at the prevailing rate.

The Lake View Country Club will not assume any responsibility for the damage or loss of any merchandise or articles left on the property prior to during or following the scheduled function.

Special services such as electrical connections, plumbing, staging, special lighting and others will be charged at the prevailing schedule. Direct shipments, special handling, set up of displays, etc. must be pre-arranged with the Sales Department. Coordination and charges of storage, loading, unloading and exhibit set ups is the responsibility of the patron. Failure to notify the Lake View Country Club can result in refusal of shipments and/or additional charges to the patron.

The delivery of cakes, flowers, etc. must be pre-arranged with the Sales Department three days in advance of the event.

Patron agrees to be responsible for any damage done to the premises during the period of time they are under your control, or the control of any independent contractors as contracted by patron.

It is specifically understood that decorations, signing and other such and similar items will not be attached in any manner to the walls, doors or structure of any part of the building.

Failure to vacate the premises in a neat and clean condition, requiring only vacuuming, no later than the date and time agreed upon, will authorize the Lake View Country Club to charge the Association or the patron labor charges for the removal of decoration, exhibit or display refuse.

Any intended use of audio-visual equipment must be arranged for with the Sales Department three days prior to your event. Sales Office must be notified 48 hours in advance for any cancellation of equipment. You will be charged for any lost or stolen equipment rented for your event.

Performance of this agreement is contingent upon the ability of the Lake View Country Club Management to complete the same, and is subject to the labor troubles, disputes or strikes, accidents, governmental (Federal, State, or Municipal) regulations, restrictions upon travel, transportation, foods and beverages or supplies and other causes whether enumerated herein or not, beyond control of Management, preventing or interfering with performance. In no event shall the Lake View Country Club be liable for loss of profit or for other similar or dissimilar collateral or consequential damages whether based on breach of contract, warranty or otherwise.

All notices shall be to the Lake View Country Club, c/o Sales and Catering, N78 W28050 Lakeview Drive, Bristol, WA 78092, which is open for business from 9 o'clock a.m. to 5 o'clock p.m., Monday through Friday, and to customer at the address shown on the reverse hereof.

Prices are quoted on a cash basis. Payment by credit card will be subject to an additional 5% financial service charge.

The Country Club must be permitted a 15 minute period for clearing of tables immediately following your meal.

Please note that we do not allow picture taking on the golf course or practice green. We ask that any outdoor photography be held to the immediate perimeter of the club house.

Reception Guide
SITE COMPARISONS

LOCATION	1	2	3
Name			
Phone			
Manager			
Date			
Time			
Address			
Date Available/Number of Guests			
Ample Parking			
Menu Selection (Rate 1–5)			
Food Quality (Fair, Good Excellent)			
Wait Staff Provided			
Air-Conditioning			
Linens/Napkins			
Cake Table			
Public Address System			
Piano			
Dance Floor			
Power Outlets			
Tables and Chairs			
Coat Room			
Full Bar Facilities			
Decorations Allowed			
Cleanup Requirements			
Deposit Required Cancellation Fee			
General Rating (1–5)			

Reception Guideline
OUR RECEPTION WORKSHEET

Our Selected Site _____

Address _____

Site Coordinator _____   Phone (_____) - _____

Confirmed Date _____   Time _____ to _____

Room Reserved _____

Deposit Paid _____   Date _____

Balance Amount _____   Date Due _____

Cancellation Policy _____

Last date to give final head count _____

RECEPTION FACILITY LAYOUT

Cut out pieces below and design your own reception layout.

Once you know the approximate number of guests, you will be able to calculate the number of tables needed—allowing 8 or 10 guests per table. Keep open space around bar, buffet, rest rooms and entrances. Dance floor and entertainment should be centrally located. Cake table should be visible to all for cake cutting ceremony. Arrange the head table to be within view of all guest tables. Reserve tables for the immediate families and place them adjacent to head table.

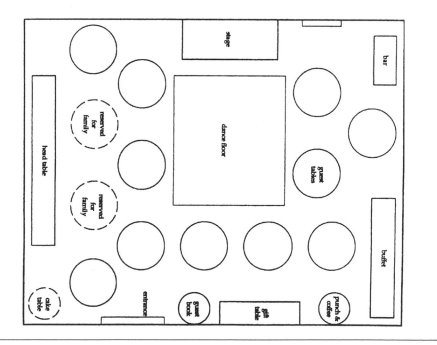

Reception Guideline
MISCELLANEOUS WEDDING DUTIES

Allow your attendants, ushers, family and friends to help you by performing special wedding duties that you should not do yourself.

SPECIAL TASK	PERFORMED BY
Help set up entertainment/equipment	
Distribute ceremony programs	
Help videographer	
Guest book signing	
Ring pillow arrangements	
Pay clergyman	
Pass out birdseed to toss	
Set up gift table	
Arrange place cards/special seating	
Carry bridal first-aid kit	
Move gifts after reception	
Bring unity candle	
Give fee to musicians	
Pay reception balance	
Move top layer of cake	
Store cake in freezer	
Collect extra favors/accessories	
Take wedding gown to cleaners	
Return groom's tuxedo	
Take bouquet to be preserved	
Develop film	
Drive wedding couple to airport	
Deposit money in bank	
Watch house while honeymooning	
Cut announcement out of paper	
Return any rental equipment	

CATERING GUIDELINE

Your wedding meal is the centerpiece of your reception party. While it shows your good taste, it also is the first thing your guests will complain about. It is wise, therefore, to know how to make sure the food is fabulous, but does *not* cost you a fortune.

Shop around. Ask to taste samples when you meet with prospective caterers. Compare costs and keep notes on the cost comparison page in this chapter. I've included a sample catering contract for you to review. Read over this typical contract and its terms. Ask your caterer of choice for a copy of their contract. Take it home and review it carefully. If you have questions or disagree with any of the terms, discuss them with your caterer and make adjustments (*in writing*) on the contract so that you feel secure and pleased with the agreement. Remember, too, that both you *and* your caterer should sign the agreement. This makes the terms of the agreement binding on *both* parties.

I have also included a beverage worksheet because most people do not know how to estimate how much their guests will drink. You will find this information to be extremely helpful in controlling your refreshment costs.

Wedding accessories give a final touch to your wedding reception. Because many of the items can be included as table and room decorations, I have featured them in this chapter. Also consider using balloons. They are economical, colorful and can fill an otherwise empty-looking banquet room.

Notes about

THE CATERING

Catering Guideline
VENDOR INFORMATION

WHEN TO MAKE ARRANGEMENTS

Choosing the right caterer is *most* important because your guests will either complain all evening about how bad their food was or long remember how wonderful it was.

Meet with prospective caterers no sooner than one year and no later than nine months before your wedding day.

Final menu selection is usually decided one month before your date.

WHERE TO FIND THE BEST

You can look for caterers in your local yellow pages directory, but the smart way to learn who are the best is to ask friends or coworkers, or to ask for business cards at banquets or holiday parties you attend where the food was outstanding.

WHAT TO WATCH OUT FOR

- Be sure to ask the caterer for a printed price list of their appetizer and entrée selections. Any reputable caterer will readily provide a menu of selections like this.
- Remember—catering professionals will work creatively to customize a menu to help their clients stay within their budgets.

WHAT IT WILL COST

Some caterers charge a flat rate ($1,000 for serving 100 people). Most caterers charge on a per-person basis. (National average rates range between $15 to $50 per person.) Your estimated bill should be in *writing.* Be sure all extras, such as cake cutting fees or serving gratuities, are added to this bill estimate. Otherwise, you will be unhappily surprised with the add-on charges on your final bill. Expect to pay a deposit of 25% of the total bill when you sign your catering contract.

A WEDDING CUSTOM OR TRADITION

At your reception, consider presenting each guest with a wedding favor—a tulle-wrapped bundle of sugared almonds. Italian tradition says that this confection represents both the sweetness and bitterness of married life.

A Wedding Wi$e Tip

Many brides have reported that they receive a 10–15% discount off their final bill when they brought another client to the caterer. Caterers depend on word-of-mouth advertising, and you can profit, too.

IMPORTANT
FACTS
TO KNOW

1. Your reception meal accounts for 35% of your *entire* wedding costs!

2. All wedding meals served before 3:00 P.M. are considered a luncheon. Plan your meal before that time and save up to 30%.

3. A sit-down dinner features a meal of portioned foods already assembled on a plate that is served to seated guests.

4. A buffet dinner can be

   • one long table of serving dishes and platters of food from which guests serve themselves

   • a group of "station tables," each station featuring different meal components. One may contain salads, pastas, and vegetables. Another may be the dessert station. You can even feature a chef hand-carving roast beef for your guests.

5. Some reception sites provide in-house catering that you must use as part of your reception contract. Other sites will allow you to bring in your own caterer, or will supply you with a list of recommended professionals with whom they have successfully dealt in the past.

6. Your catering contract should specify *all* food items that will be served—*plus* the number of wait staff that will serve it.

7. A 15–20% wait-staff gratuity will automatically be added to your total food bill.

8. The Better Business Bureau can tell you if any complaints or charges have been registered against any caterers you may be considering.

9. Protect yourself—pay your catering deposit with a credit card. In that way, if you have any problems, your credit card company will stand behind you and retrieve your deposit money for you, if necessary.

Catering Guideline
SAMPLE CATERING ORDER

Date: _____

Wedding Name: _____

Wedding Date: _____

Reception Site:

Manager: _____

Address: _____

City: _____ State: _____ Zip: _____

Phone: _____

House of Epicurean Delight

CATERING ORDER

Menu	Quantity Ordered	Description	Price	Per	Total

TOTAL PRICE _____

Deposit _____

Balance Due _____

Payment Schedule _____

_____

Cancellation or Refund policy (on front or back side)
READ THEIR POLICY—If you do not agree with something, put a line through it.
(This means that it will not apply in your invitation agreement.)

Buyer _____ *For Seller* _____
BE SURE they sign, too!

Catering Guideline
COST COMPARISONS

LOCATION	1	2	3
Caterer			
Address			
Phone			
Representative			
MENU			
Hors D'oeuvres			
Appetizers			
Soup/Salad			
Main Course #1 Main Course #2			
Side Dishes Potatoes Vegetables Relishes Jell-O Bread/Rolls Beverages Desserts Cake Cutting Fee			
Per Person Rate			
Flat Rate			
Deposit			
Cancellation Terms			
Balance Due			

Catering Guideline
BEVERAGE WORKSHEET

1. Today both alcoholic and nonalcoholic beverages are served at weddings.
2. The number one toasting beverage is champagne. You can also use sparkling cider or white wine. Nonalcoholic toasting beverages include ginger ale, bubbling punch, club soda and white grape juice.
3. Children will drink approximately 3 glasses of soda per hour.
4. The later the reception time, the more guests will drink.

> A party guest will consume approximately 2 drinks during the first hour and 1 drink each hour following.

5. As a courtesy, offer coffee during the last hour of the reception.

OUR BAR SERVICE

	Cost
Champagne:	
Wine: Red White	
Beer:	
Soda:	
Liquors: _____ _____ _____ _____	
Mixers: _____ _____ _____ _____	
OPEN BAR COST Bar open from: _____ to _____ Estimated No. of Guests: _____ How charged?_____ Estimated Cost: _____	
CASH BAR COST Bar open from: _____ to _____ Estimated No. of Guests: _____ How charged?_____ Estimated Cost: _____	
DINNER Is bar to be closed during meal? _____ Beverages served during dinner? _____	

Catering Guideline
ACCESSORIES AND FAVORS

ACCESSORIES TO CONSIDER

Unity candle and base
Wedding programs
Ring pillow
Guest book
Cake-top keepsake
Cake knife
Toasting goblets
Out-of-town guest hospitality baskets
Ice sculpture
Decorative envelope gift holder
Champagne fountain
Mirrored table centers
Napkin rings
Single-use cameras

FAVOR IDEAS
CANDY/COOKIE/FOOD IDEAS

Tulle-wrapped candied almonds
Small gift boxes of chocolates
Personalized foiled-wrapped
    chocolates
"Poppers"—a paper confection that
    "pops" open and is candy filled
Sugar cookies cut into shapes of bells
    or wedding cakes, hand frosted
Bubble gum brides and grooms

FLOWERS

Breakaway centerpieces
Mini bud vases with fresh flowers at
    each place setting
A rose or carnation at each place
    setting

MISCELLANEOUS

Packets of flower seeds
Birdseed roses
Miniature bottles of wine with
    personalized labels
Handpainted easter eggs with couples
    initials
Cakes of scented soaps
A special engraved Christmas
    ornament

Catering Guideline
BALLOON DECORATIONS

Balloons create a festive party atmosphere. Alone or combined with flowers, balloons have become the most popular and economical form of wedding decoration.

CEREMONY

Altar arrangements: _____

Colors used: _____

Number needed: _____ Cost: $_____

Pew marker arrangements: _____

Colors/Kinds used: _____

Number needed: _____ Cost: $_____

RECEPTION

Head table decorations: _____

Colors used: _____

Number needed: _____ Cost: $_____

Guest table decorations: _____

Colors/Kinds used: _____

Number needed: _____ Cost: $_____

Buffet table decorations: _____

Colors/Kinds used: _____

Number needed: _____ Cost: $_____

Balloon Arches: _____

Color/Kinds used: _____

Balloon Envelope Holder: _____

Color/Kinds used: _____

Special Balloon Decorations:

_____ Colors: _____

_____ Colors: _____

DELIVERY

Date: _____ Time: _____ Address: _____

Total Cost of balloons and balloon arrangements: _____

ENTERTAINMENT GUIDELINE

Because the reception entertainment can make or break your celebration party, hiring only the *best* should be your *top* priority. Today both live bands and DJs have reference networks. These printed booklets provide up-to-date listings of existing groups in your area—both for ceremonies and receptions. They include names, addresses and full descriptions of the group's service and fees. These booklets are available at local wedding retailers or on the Internet.

For your ceremony: I have included a music schedule in this chapter. It will aid you and your group of choice in deciding what musical selections you wish to use.

For your reception: Before you decide, review the convenient chart comparing DJs and live bands. Also review the reception outline. It will help you to organize all of the precious traditional ''reception activities'' as well as the favorite dance tunes that you will want to include. Don't forget to consider the ethnic customs and novel new wedding entertainment ideas in this chapter.

Above all, *shop around*. Compare ideas and costs, keep notes and *read the contract*. I've included a sample entertainment contract for you to review. Read over this typical contract and its terms. Ask your group of choice for a copy of their contract. Take it home and review it carefully. If you have questions or disagree with any of the terms, discuss them with your group and make adjustments (*in writing*) on the contract so that you feel secure and pleased with the agreement. Remember, too, that both you *and* your group manager should sign your agreement. This makes the terms of the agreement binding on *both* parties.

Notes about

THE ENTERTAINMENT

CEREMONY

RECEPTION

Entertainment Guideline
VENDOR INFORMATION

WHEN TO MAKE ARRANGEMENTS

The most important part of your reception party is your entertainment.
Bored guests will not stay but will remember the poor entertainment.
Make your choices as soon as possible since popular qualified entertainers are booked up to one year in advance.

WHERE TO FIND THE BEST

Check yellow pages for entertainment bands, band agencies and band unions.
Ask friends or relatives for references.
Reception managers can also recommend local entertainers.
Many cities offer DJ and band referral networks that provide a free up-to-date listing of local talents.

WHAT TO WATCH OUT FOR

• Personally audition the bands you like by viewing them at another wedding.

WHAT IT WILL COST

Always *comparison shop*—bands are competitive.
Ask for references.
A DJ band charges between $300 and $750.

A live band costs between $500 and $8,000 (depending on number of musicians in group).

Live bands also charge an overtime fee of $25–$100 *per musician*, per hour.

A WEDDING CUSTOM OR TRADITION

Guests at many Mexican weddings still observe an entertainment tradition in which they gather around the wedding couple in a heart-shaped ring as the couple whirls through their first dance as husband and wife.

A Wedding Wi$e Tip

Be specific about fees for any musical entertainment, and *bring your contract* with you to your wedding. The element of time is an important factor. If your band is scheduled for 7:00 P.M. but does not arrive, deduct a percentage of your contract price for each 10 minutes they delay your reception celebration.

IMPORTANT FACTS TO KNOW

1. Always discuss your ceremony music with your officiant. Some churches have restrictions about other instruments and song selections.
2. Get references and check them.
3. Listen to musicians perform. Ask if they have an audiotape.
4. Some ceremony musical groupings to consider:

   Pianist or organist with a vocalist
   Harpist
   Brass quartet
   Flute or other soft musical combinations

5. Ceremony musicians continue to play while your guests depart from the church, which completes this special effect.

Entertainment Guideline
SAMPLE CONTRACT

UE UNIVERSAL ENTERTAINMENT

CONTRACT BLANK

THIS CONTRACT for the personal services of musicians on the engagement described below, made this _____ day of _____ 19 _____, between the undersigned Purchaser of Music (herein called "Employer") and _____ musicians.*
(including leader)

The musicians are engaged severally on the terms and conditions on the face and reverse sides hereof. The leader represents that the musicians already designated have agreed to be bound by said terms and conditions. Each musician yet to be chosen, upon acceptance, shall be bound by said terms and conditions. Each musician may enforce this agreement. The musicians severally agree to render services under the undersigned leader.

1. Name and Address of Place of Engagement _____

_____

2. Date(s), starting and finishing time of engagement _____

_____

3. Type of Engagement (specify whether dance, stage show, banquet, club, etc.

DEPOSIT RECEIVED
DATE:
Amount:

Names of Musicians

4. _____
Leader

_____

_____

_____

5. Employer will make payments, as follows: _____

_____

(Specify when payments are to be made)

6. The Employer is hereby given an option to extend this agreement for a period of _____ weeks beyond the original term thereof. Said option can be exercised only by written notice from the Employer to the musicians, not later than _____ days prior to the expiration of the original term.

(continued)

7. The Employer shall at all times have complete supervision, direction and control over the services of musicians on the engagement and expressly reserves the right to control the manner, means and details of the performance of services by the musicians including the leader as well as the ends to be accomplished. If any musicians have not been chosen upon the signing of this contract, the leader shall, as agent for the Employer and under his instructions, hire such persons and any replacements as are required.

8. In accordance, the parties will submit every claim, dispute, controversy or difference involving the musical services arising out of or connected with this contract and the engagement covered thereby for determination by the International Arbitration Board or an appropriate local thereof and such determination shall be conclusive, final and binding upon the parties.

ADDITIONAL TERMS AND CONDITIONS

The leader shall, as agent of the Employer, enforce disciplinary measures for just cause, and carry out instructions as to selections and manner of performance. The agreement of the musicians to perform is subject to proven detention by sickness, accidents, riots, strikes, epidemics, acts of God, or any other legitimate conditions beyond their control. On behalf of the Employer the leader will distribute the amount received from the Employer to the musicians, including himself, as indicated on this contract, or in place thereof on separate memorandum supplied to the Employer at or before the commencement of the employment hereunder and take and turn over to the Employer receipts therefor from each musician, including himself. The amount paid to the leader includes the cost of transportation, which will be reported by the leader to the Employer.

Any musicians on the engagement are free to cease service hereunder by reason of any strike, ban, unfair list order and shall be free to accept and engage in other employment of the same or similar character or otherwise, without any restraint, hindrance, penalty, obligation or liability whatever, any other provisions of this contract to the contrary notwithstanding.

No performance on the engagement shall be recorded, reproduced or transmitted from the place of performance, in any manner or by any means whatsoever, in the absence of a specific written agreement with the Federation relating to and permitting such recording, reproduction or transmission.

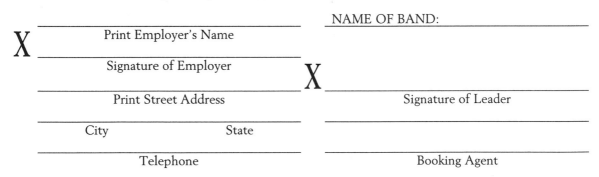

NAME OF BAND:

X _____
   Print Employer's Name

   _____
   Signature of Employer

   _____   X _____
   Print Street Address   Signature of Leader

   _____
   City   State

   _____   _____
   Telephone   Booking Agent

*This contract does not conclusively determine the person liable to report and pay employment taxes and similar employer levies under rulings of the U.S. Internal Revenue Service and of some state agencies.

Entertainment Guideline
COST COMPARISONS

LIVE MUSIC ESTIMATE #1	MOBILE MUSIC ESTIMATE #1	MISCELLANEOUS ESTIMATE #1
Group Name _____	Group Name _____	Group Name _____
Contact Person _____	Contact Person _____	Contact Person _____
Address _____	Address _____	Address _____
Phone _____	Phone _____	Phone _____
# in Group _____	# in Group _____	# in Group _____
Specialty Features	Specialty Features	Specialty Features
_____	_____	_____
_____	_____	_____
_____	_____	_____
FEE _____	FEE _____	FEE _____

LIVE MUSIC ESTIMATE #2	MOBILE MUSIC ESTIMATE #2	MISCELLANEOUS ESTIMATE #2
Group Name _____	Group Name _____	Group Name _____
Contact Person _____	Contact Person _____	Contact Person _____
Address _____	Address _____	Address _____
Phone _____	Phone _____	Phone _____
# in Group _____	# in Group _____	# in Group _____
Specialty Features	Specialty Features	Specialty Features
_____	_____	_____
_____	_____	_____
_____	_____	_____
FEE _____	FEE _____	FEE _____

LIVE MUSIC ESTIMATE #3	MOBILE MUSIC ESTIMATE #3	MISCELLANEOUS ESTIMATE #3
Group Name _____	Group Name _____	Group Name _____
Contact Person _____	Contact Person _____	Contact Person _____
Address _____	Address _____	Address _____
Phone _____	Phone _____	Phone _____
# in Group _____	# in Group _____	# in Group _____
Specialty Features	Specialty Features	Specialty Features
_____	_____	_____
_____	_____	_____
_____	_____	_____
FEE _____	FEE _____	FEE _____

Entertainment Guideline
CEREMONY MUSIC SCHEDULE

Remove and make copies for the musicians, vocalists or church organist.

Wedding of _____

Date _____

Time _____

Church _____

Address _____

OUR CEREMONY MUSIC SELECTIONS

1. Prelude_____
   a._____
   b._____
   c._____

2. Seating of Parents _____

3. Processional _____

4. Bride's Entrance _____

5. Reading I _____

6. Reading II _____

7. Vows/Exchange of Rings _____

8. Candle Lighting _____

9. Communion _____

10. Recessional _____

11. Postlude (as family and guests exit) _____

12. Other _____

_____

_____

Entertainment Guideline
RECEPTION MUSIC OPTIONS

The average performance time for musical entertainment is four hours. While it is not necessary to tip the band, many couples provide a meal to the group before they begin to play.

DJ	LIVE BAND
• 4-hour appearance time	• 4-hour appearance time
• CDs or stereo equipment	• *Live* instruments and vocalist
• Brings library of musical selections	• Plays big variety but may not know all songs
• Provides *continuous* music	• One 15-minute break per hour
• Offers original songs played as guests remember them.	• Plays in their own style and may use different versions of melodies
• *Key* is hiring a skilled, lively announcer	• Band leader should be a great master of ceremonies
• Extra equipment—laser lights, strobes, glass ball, others—ensure entertaining evening of fun.	• Live vocalist adds glamorous touch to entertainment
• Minimal space required for operation	• Size requirement varies by number of musicians in group (4–5 is average)
• Cost ranges between $300 and $750	• Costs range between $500 and $8,000

Entertainment Guideline
OUR RECEPTION OUTLINE

(Remove and make copies of this schedule. Give to the entertainment leader to be sure your bridal party and other important people will be included in your reception festivities. Fill in names and special songs you want included.)

Activity	Timeline	People Included	Music Selection
Cocktail hour			
During receiving line			
Bridal party entrance			
Toasts to be made			
During meal			
First dance (your favorite song)		Bride and groom	
		Bride's parents	
		Groom's parents	
		Maid of honor	
		Best man	
		Groomsman	
		Bridesmaid	
		Groomsman	
		Bridesmaid	
		Groomsman	
		Bridesmaid	
		Groomsman	
		Bridesmaid	
		Groomsman	
		Bridesmaid	
		Groomsman	
		Bridesmaid	
Father/Bride dance			
Mother/Groom dance			
Special opening mixer			
Special ethnic dance			
Line dances			
Cake cutting			
Bouquet throw			
Garter toss			
Farewell dance			

Entertainment Guideline
RECEPTION FESTIVITIES

Special customs continue to be an integral part of a traditional wedding celebration. Consider some or all of the following to make your wedding a symbolic rite of passage.

THE RECEIVING LINE

The receiving line is an official lineup of the important people of the wedding party. Today, it is usually the wedding couple and their parents, who greet and introduce friend and relatives.

THE WEDDING TOAST

The wedding toast is made by the best man before the meal is served. This toast salutes the couple and wishes them a lifetime of happiness. It can be funny and sentimental but should never be embarrassing to either the bride or groom.

THE FIRST DANCE

The entertainer/master of ceremonies directs all attention to the dance floor as the bride and groom make their way to the center. "Their song" begins and the announcer presents them as husband and wife. The guests cheer and applaude. Halfway through the song, the parents and other party members are introduced and join in the dancing. Grandparents do not have to be included in this dance.

THE WEDDING CAKE CUTTING

This wedding custom symbolizes the couple's commitment to share their worldly goods. Cutting the cake, his hand over hers, and feeding each other a piece of it, is said to ensure their future happiness.

BOUQUET THROW

This event is for the benefit of the single women at the wedding. All gather into the center of the dance floor and circle around the bride. Bride may or may not be blindfolded, and throws her bouquet over her shoulder. It is said that the one who catches the bouquet will be the next to marry.

GARTER THROW

This custom allows the groom to remove the garter from the bride's left leg and toss it over his shoulder to all the single men, who have encircled him.

THE LAST DANCE

Once again the wedding couple dances alone in the center of the dance floor to "their song." Reception guests are then directed to form a circle of love around them. When music ends, all can applaud, or the dance can be followed by a shower of confetti, rose petals or birdseed as the couple exits to their car.

ETHNIC CUSTOMS TO CONSIDER

Detailed information about individual nationalities and their customs can be found at your local library, or through local ethnic community centers, but here are some suggestions:

• The Grand March, an Italian wedding custom
• The Dollar Dance, an Olde Polish wedding dance
• The Greek Handkerchief Dance
• The Jewish Horah Dance
• The Italian Tarantella Folk Dance

❧

NEW WEDDING FESTIVITIES IDEAS

Today, couples of the nineties want their wedding to be *different*. Novel entertainment is one of the ways they surprise their guests and create a wedding to remember. Following are some unique ideas to consider:

• A fortune-teller or psychic
• A handwriting analyst
• Mimes in costume
• Professional dancers to perform ethnic folk dances
• Laser light show
• A slide show—video biography combining home movies, snapshots, etc., of couple as they grew, met, became engaged and planned the wedding (a 15-minute presentation)
• A fireworks display
• Single-use cameras on tables
• Pianist only featuring background music of Broadway show tunes.

PHOTOGRAPHY GUIDELINE

The longest-lasting memory of your entire wedding day will be your wedding photographs. Because of this, your choice of how, and who, to capture those images should be a very important consideration.

In this chapter, you will find important facts that will aid you in selecting the perfect professional for you. Remember capturing a moment that is flattering to the subjects, and tells the story as well, requires much more than just clicking a shutter.

Shop around. Don't feel shy about interviewing two or three photographers. Professional photographers will be pleased with your interest, and will respect your desire to look around before you decide. Take notes and compare them with the comparison page in this chapter. Be sure to make notes about any special-effects photographs or other unique photography styles you see and like.

I've included a sample photography contract for you to review. Read over this typical contract and its terms. Ask your photographer of choice for a copy of his or her contract. Take it home and review it carefully. If you have questions or disagree with any of the terms, discuss them with your photographer and make adjustments (*in writing*) on the contract so that you feel secure and pleased with the agreement. Remember, too, that both you *and* your photographer should sign your agreement. This makes the terms of the agreement binding on *both* parties.

A professional photographer will bring sensitivity and skill to your wedding. Follow the guidelines in this chapter and you will have a treasure of wedding memories that you can cherish always.

Notes about

THE PHOTOGRAPHER

Photography Guideline
VENDOR INFORMATION

WHEN TO MAKE ARRANGEMENTS

Begin to shop *immediately* after you have reserved your reception site. Today, it is not uncommon to find that quality wedding photographers have advance bookings for one year or more.

WHERE TO FIND THE BEST

Most full-service photographers can be found through personal references or bridal shows.

They can also be recommended by reception managers, caterers or florists.

WHAT TO WATCH OUT FOR

• Sales tax is applicable on a photographer's bill. Make sure you are told what your *total* cost will be.

WHAT IT WILL COST

Wedding photography can be sold as a "package" or on an hourly rate basis.
Expect to pay a deposit of one-third to one-half down when signing the contract.
Pay the balance *only* upon receipt of your finished prints.
Photography pricing varies in every city in America. Today, the national average cost for a wedding photographer for approximately a 4-hour time period, with a package of twenty-four 5×7 color prints is $1,000.

A WEDDING CUSTOM OR TRADITION

Attaching a "Just Married" sign to the back of your car and tying old shoes that dangle behind the car (as is done in England) signifies recognition of the creation of a new family unit. Be sure your photographer captures this unique decoration if you include it in your wedding day plans.

A Wedding Wi$e Tip

Protect your wedding pictures forever. Have your wedding photo negatives printed on a CD-ROM.
They will never fade or tear.
Twenty years from now, your wedding pictures will look as bright and beautiful as the day on which they were taken.

IMPORTANT FACTS TO KNOW

1. Personally visit and interview at least 2–3 photographers. Look at their sample albums and decide if you like their photographic style.
2. Photography can be purchased as a package or at an hourly rate. Be sure to investigate the cost differences. In some situations, you may actually save money by hiring the photographer only for a specific time period.
3. Professional Digital Imaging is computer-based equipment that many professional photographers now use in their high-tech photo processing labs. This process allows a photographer to virtually create a perfect picture *every* time! It's amazing. Ask your potential photographers about it.
4. The new look in photo albums today is "old." Antique finishes and engraved covers provide an elegant cocktail table book for your home or apartment. To complete the look, you can have your wedding pictures processed in "brown and white," giving them a nostalgic 1900s finish.
5. Black-and-white wedding photographs are a trendy idea now. They are also an economical one—saving you as much as 30%. Plus, these photographs feature dramatic contrasts and can provide a modern high-tech look.
6. Special-effects photography is in great demand for wedding albums. Open any album and you will find at least one picture in which a split frame, a filter or a multiple exposure has produced a very beautiful and unique wedding photograph.
7. A good photographer will always want to be present at your wedding rehearsal if he or she has never been to the site before. During this time, the photographer will explore the location and plan his or her camera setup.
8. The very best wedding photographer is a professional who handles the assignment fully, yet never seems to be in the way.

Photography Guideline
SAMPLE CONTRACT

PICTURE PERFECT   Wedding Date: _____

ORDER # _____

Bride's Name _____ Home Phone _____

Groom's Name _____ Home Phone _____

Arrival Time _____ Total Shooting Time _____

Bride's Address _____ Dressing At _____

Church Name _____ Address _____

Special Events _____

Time of Reception _____ Place _____

Size of Party: Bride & Groom + _____ couples, + _____
Newspaper Photo ☐ Send to_____
Album Style _____
Mileage Charge _____ Overtime Charges _____
Package Selected (Write out everything) _____

_____

_____

_____

_____

_____

_____

_____

TOTAL PRICE _____

DEPOSIT _____

BALANCE DUE _____

<u>PAYMENT SCHEDULE</u> _____

_____

Cancellation or Refund Policy (on front or back side)
READ THEIR POLICY—If you do not agree with something, put a line through it.
(This means that it will not apply in your invitation agreement.)

*Buyer*_____ *For Seller*_____
BE SURE they sign, too!

(continued)

CONTRACT TERMS

1. A $100 deposit must be paid when signing contract or within one week of that date. A total amount of $_____ must be paid at least *two weeks prior* to the wedding date. PICTURE PERFECT Photographers will not be bound until prior conditions are met. In the event of a date change, the money will be applied to a new date if there is an opening. Times and date changes must be acceptable to both parties.

2. If a cancellation takes place, anytime prior to six weeks before the wedding date, a minimum deposit of 1/2 full plan will be due and retained by PICTURE PERFECT. If the cancellation occurs within six weeks of the wedding date, the total amount of the plan will be due and retained by PICTURE PERFECT for date reservation and booking services.

3. All original negatives and prints are the exclusive property of PICTURE PERFECT Photography and may be used in their advertising or display promotions.

4. No negatives or prints may be used, copied or kept without the studio's permission. No liability is assumed if any film, prints, slides or original negatives are damaged, lost or destroyed as a result of fire, theft, accident or any cause whatsoever.

5. PICTURE PERFECT Photography guarantees that all money paid will be refunded should they find it necessary to cancel this contract and assumes no other liability. No *one* photographer is guaranteed to perform the contracted services: that is PICTURE PERFECT reserves the right to assign any of their photographers to fulfill this contract.

6. No professional photographs may be used in a slide program or video transfer without the written permission of the photographer. (Violation of Photographer Copyright)

7. Our photographers must have full control of the wedding photographs. We are hereby granted exclusive rights to photograph alone.

8. All charges and costs for prints and albums must be paid in full and picked up on scheduled delivery date, as one complete order by the contracting party signed on the front of this agreement.

Photography Guideline
COST COMPARISONS

LOCATION	1	2	3
Photographer Name			
Phone			
Contact Person			
Date			
Appointment Time			
Address			
Hours Open			
Wedding Album Packages			
#1 Description, Cost			
#2 Description, Cost			
Hourly Rate			
Special Effects			
Environmental Photos			
# of Proofs			
# of Prints			
Size of Prints			
Additional Prints			
Travel Costs			
Portraits: Engagement—Cost Bridal—Cost			
Prints for Newspaper			
Deposit Required			
Balance Due When			
Payment Plans			

VIDEO GUIDELINE

While your photographer is the director of your love story, it is the videographer who is the cameraman filming all the important sights and sounds of your day. This chapter contains important facts that you can review in selecting the best professional for this most important movie of your life.

Visit several videographers. At the meeting, view video samples of their previous work. Discuss the different styles of videos that I have described in this chapter. Your video costs will be determined by the style you choose.

Take notes and compare costs as well as all the special features that each offers. Remember, when comparing prices, make sure you are comparing similar plans. Keep track of all with the cost comparison page in this chapter.

I have also included a sample videography contract for you to review. Read over this typical contract and its terms. Ask your videographer of choice for a copy of his or her contract. Take it home and review it carefully. If you have questions or disagree with any of the terms, discuss them with your videographer and make adjustments (*in writing*) on the contract so that you feel secure and pleased with the agreement. Remember, too, that both you *and* your videographer should sign your agreement. This makes the terms of the agreement binding on *both* parties.

Best Advice: Remember to *keep smiling*. The ''perfect'' wedding video is one that exudes the joy and delight of newlyweds sharing their day with grand smiles.

Notes about

THE VIDEO

Video Guideline
VENDOR INFORMATION

WHEN TO MAKE ARRANGEMENTS

Reserve your videographer no later than six months before your wedding day, but *not* before you contract with your wedding photographer. A videographer records all of the moving sights and sounds of this precious celebration, but it is the photographer who captures the moments that are worth a thousand words.

Sometimes photographers will recommend videographers with whom they have worked well at previous weddings. You don't want people to be stepping on each other's toes.

❧

WHERE TO FIND THE BEST

Today, 60%–80% of wedding couples have their wedding videotaped. Professional wedding videographers can be found by:
Personal recommendation by friends or relatives
References from reception site coordinators
Personal viewing at bridal shows
Through other couple's wedding videos

❧

WHAT TO WATCH OUT FOR

- Your videographer should have equipment that will work well in "low light" settings, enabling him or her to capture good images in poor light conditions such as candlelight ceremonies or evening dancing.

❧

WHAT IT WILL COST

There are various styles of videos. Your costs will depend on which one you select:
- *Nostalgic video*—incorporates music and photos of couple as children, through courtship and during wedding planning. Approximate cost: $1,000 or more.
- *Documentary video*—uses only wedding day scenes; shows behind-the-scenes footage of bride at home, vows at altar, and interviews and testimonials from family and friends. Approximate cost: $500–$700.
- *Straight shot video*—uses only one camera, simple stills of couple and their printed wedding date are usually included, with a musical introduction. Approximate cost: $200–$400.

❧

A WEDDING CUSTOM OR TRADITION

A modern American wedding trend is to choose a wedding site that reflects the couples' interests and provides an appropriate setting for their storybook marriage. A ski slope, a baseball stadium or a cliff overlooking water are a few ideas.

❧

A Wedding Wi$e Tip

Rent a home-to-video transferrer
(available at local camera stores).
Create your own video introduction
of baby and growing photos of
yourselves, as well as photos
of your dating years. Simply add your
intro to the wedding video and
save yourself about $150.

**IMPORTANT
FACTS
TO KNOW**

1. Your wedding video is the moving story of your love. It can include childhood photos, dating photos and photos taken during your engagement and wedding planning time. Some couples even add their honeymoon video to make the story complete.
2. Comparison shop—vendors are competitive and some will include special effects at no extra charge with their package. Be sure to look around before you decide.
3. Most quality videographers now use two cameras for the wedding ceremony. One is directed on the wedding couple, while the other films the guests and is ready for your wedding recessional.
4. Be sure to discuss your ceremony site and any restrictions that your church requires for videotaping.
5. You can make your own prewedding video by putting together footage from all of your pre-wedding parties. These include your engagement party, bridal showers and bachelor party, as well as the wedding rehearsal and rehearsal dinner party.

Video Guideline
SAMPLE VIDEOGRAPHY CONTRACT

IMAGES
Video Weddings

AGREEMENT FOR WEDDING VIDEOTAPE

Bride's Name _____   Groom's Name _____

Address _____   Home Phone _____

Arrival Time _____   Total Shooting Time _____

Church Name _____   Address _____

Time of Reception _____   Place _____

Mileage Charge _____   Overtime Charges _____

Package Selected (Write out everything)

_____

_____

_____

_____

_____

_____

_____

_____

_____

_____

All terms of this agreement have been read, are understood, and agreed upon.

IMAGES _____

Contracting Party _____   Date _____

Wedding Package & Price _____

Deposit Required _____

Tax Applied _____

Total Price _____

Read cancellation and refund policy (back side).
READ THEIR POLICY—If you do not agree with something, put a line through it.
(This means it will not apply to your videography contract.)

*Buyer*_____   *For Seller*_____

BE SURE they sign, too!

(continued)

TERMS OF THIS AGREEMENT

1. This constitutes an order for a wedding videotaping. Final product delivered to the address indicated to include edited master tape with music and graphic titles, as well as all unedited raw footage tapes. It is understood that a copy may be retained by IMAGES and excerpts may be used for display advertising or other promotional purposes.

2. ALL care will be taken with the raw footage tapes and finished product tapes. IMAGES limits liability for loss, damage and failure to deliver final product for any reason to the return of any and all deposits made.

3. Upon signature, IMAGES reserves the adequate equipment for the time and date agreed upon, and will not make other reservations for that equipment and for that time and date.

4. A $50.00 nonrefundable deposit is required to confirm the date booked. A deposit equal to half of the contracted package is required 30 days prior to the wedding date. Complete payment is due upon receipt of final product.

5. If the wedding and reception are to be videotaped, the contracting party will make provisions for the video photographer to eat and be seated in the main dining area with the guests. This helps to insure that important and impromptu events are not missed.

6. No professional photographs may be used in a slide program or video transfer without the written permission of the photographer. (Violation of Photographer Copyright)

7. It is understood that no video prints will be made of professionally posed shots set up by a photographer, and that videotaping of posed shots will be at the discretion of the wedding photographer.

8. Position of the cameras at the church may be determined at the discretion of the officiating party (e.g., priest, rabbi, minister).

9. A $20.00 fee is assessed for any location outside of a 25-mile radius of the IMAGES office.

Video Guideline
COST COMPARISONS

LOCATION	1	2	3
Videographer Name			
Phone			
Contact Person			
Date			
Appointment Time			
Address			
Hours Open			
Video Packages			
#1 Description, Cost			
#2 Description, Cost			
Type of Video			
Video Length			
Audio Equipment			
Special Effects			
Master Tape			
Additional Copies			
Travel Costs			
Total Cost			
Deposit Required			
Balance Due When			
Payment Plans			

Section Three

CELEBRATE

SELECT THE DISTINCTIVE

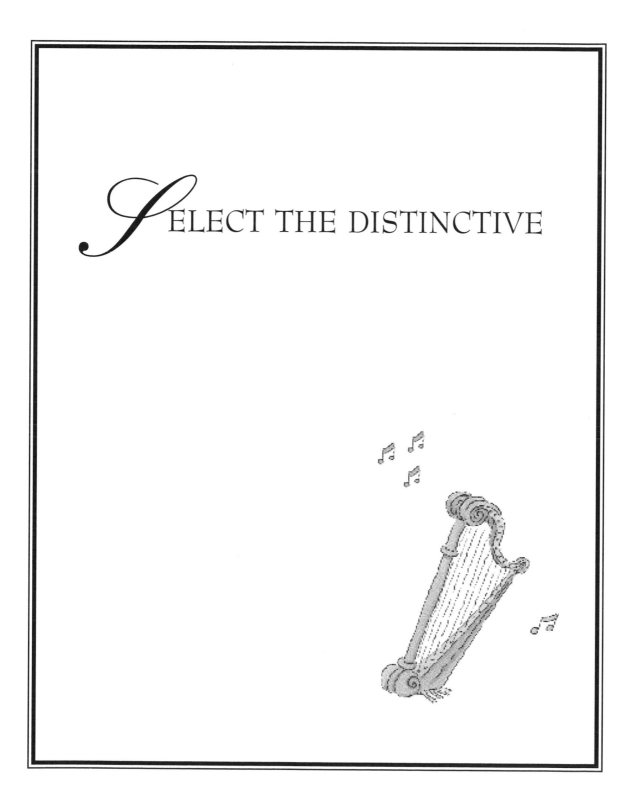

WEDDING CAKE GUIDELINE

Today, your wedding cake is not only your dessert, it also serves as the centerpiece of your reception and is usually displayed on its own decorated table. Although the most popular styles are cakes with tiers, fountains and heart shapes, the nineties brides are not necessarily following tradition when selecting the cake of their dreams. The more daring are requesting wedding cake castles, Monopoly board cakes, computer cakes and city skyline cakes for this ultimate desert. Today, a wedding cake can be *any* size and *any* shape.

As varied as the cake shapes are, so too is the selection of flavors and fillings. Most popular flavors are banana, chocolate, carrot and cheesecake. Fillings include raspberry, pineapple, fudge, butter creme and mocha. And if you're worried about your guests not sharing your tastes, ask your baker to alternate the cake flavors by tiers. Whatever your choices are, be sure to visit at least three bakers for sample tastings. Compare costs and keep notes on the page in this chapter.

I have also included a sample cake order form for you to review. Read over this typical form and its terms. Ask your baker of choice for a copy of his or her contract. Take it home and review it carefully. If you have questions or disagree with any of the terms, discuss them with your baker and make adjustments (*in writing*) on the contract so that you feel secure and pleased with the agreement. Remember, too, that both you *and* your baker should sign your agreement. This makes the terms of the agreement binding on *both* parties.

Be sure that all delivery information, including the proper address, is included on your order form. Today, most bakers send a decorator to deliver, and make any last-minute repairs, if necessary, to your cake.

Notes about

THE WEDDING CAKE

Wedding Cake Guideline
VENDOR INFORMATION

WHEN TO MAKE ARRANGEMENTS

Start shopping and tasting wedding cake no sooner than 6 months and no later than 2 months before your wedding date.

Some wedding specialty bakers limit the number of cake orders they take on a given day in order to maintain quality control.

If you're planning your wedding in a popular month (August, June, September or around any holiday), order your cake accordingly.

WHERE TO FIND THE BEST

Get recommendations from friends or relatives, or ask your reception coordinator, florist or photographer.

Local bridal magazines will give you visual ideas and local bridal shows will allow you to see and taste wedding creations.

Shop around and compare costs, taste and workmanship.

WHAT TO WATCH OUT FOR

• Today, some bakers charge by the "slice." This is especially true of cheesecakes with fruit fillings.

• Subtract 20 from your total guest count to allow for those who will not want to eat cake.

WHAT IT WILL COST

Wedding cake prices begin at $50 (a simple two-tier cake) and go up from there.

Your cake topper is also an extra charge prices range between $10 to $150.

Prepare to pay a deposit of 10% of the total cost when you order your cake.

A WEDDING CUSTOM OR TRADITION

The traditional wedding cake of Ireland is a rich fruitcake made with golden raisins, ground almonds, cherries and spices. It is also laced with bourbon or brandy. It is this cake that is given to wedding guests to take home with them as a wedding souvenir.

A Wedding Wi$e Tip

Save money by using a "home baker" who works out of his or her own kitchen. This baker will produce desserts with a home-baked flavor and freshness.

IMPORTANT
FACTS
TO KNOW

1. The most common blunder a baker can make with a wedding cake is to deliver it to the wrong wedding reception site.
2. Today, a wedding cake can be any size, shape or flavor you desire, and it usually includes your wedding colors. Be sure to shop around and compare costs.
3. Traditionally, the wedding cake has been called the "official" food of a wedding.
4. Today, a wedding cake can be seperate tiers of cakes with a different cake flavor for every tier.
5. The wedding cake can be displayed on its own decorated table at your reception.
6. The groom's cake (baked in a shape from his favorite sport or hobby—a golf course, a tennis court, a race car) has become an American wedding tradition.
7. Plastic bride and groom figurines are outdated. New trends include fresh flowers or hand-painted porcelain figurines that can be used later as decorative accessories in your home.
8. For a different wedding dessert, feature a "Viennese table" with an assortment of pastries, cookies, finger foods and miniature tarts and cakes.
9. Use a freezer-proof container to store the top layer of your wedding cake (your first anniversary cake).
10. A new wedding cake trend: Instead of saving the top layer of your wedding cake, save one bottle of your wedding champagne and use the baker's special gift certificate for a freshly baked first anniversary cake.

Wedding Cake Guideline
SAMPLE ORDER

Heavenly Wedding Cakes	
Open Seven Days a Week	
SPECIAL ORDER	Wedding Date
Bride's Name	
Address	
Home Phone	
Reception Site	
Delivery Time	
WEDDING CAKE	
Shape	
Cake Flavor	
Filling Flavor	
Icing Flavor	
Special Decorations	
GROOM'S CAKE	
Shape	
Flavor	
Size	
Icing	
EXTRAS	
Cake Knife	
Fresh Flower Trim	

Total Price _____
Deposit Required _____
Balance Due _____

Read cancellation and refund policy (back side).
READ THEIR POLICY–If you do not agree with something, put a line through it.
(This means it will not apply to your wedding cake order).

Wedding Cake Guideline
COST COMPARISONS

LOCATION	1	2	3
Bakery's Name			
Phone			
Contact Person			
Date			
Appointment Time			
Address			
Hours Open			
CAKE DESCRIPTION			
Size			
Shape			
Cake Flavor			
Frosting			
CAKE DECORATION			
Cake Top			
Cake Flowers			
Cake Stands			
GROOM'S CAKE			
Size/Shape			
Cake Flavor			
Filling			
Frosting			
CAKE ACCESSORIES			
Cake Boxes			
Cake Knife			
COSTS			
Number to Serve			
Cost per Slice			
Total Cost			
Deposit Required			
Cancellation Policy			
Balance Due When			
Deliver/Setup			

FLOWER GUIDELINE

Across America, the year-round traditional favorite wedding flowers are roses, carnations, mums and some orchid varieties. These flowers are popular because they combine well with other varieties and are durable.

When shopping for flowers, be sure to bring along a colored fabric swatch of your bridesmaids' dresses, and a sketch or photograph of your gown. Compare costs and keep your notes on the cost comparison page in this chapter. Also ask what flowers are seasonal in your area of the country. Usually seasonal flowers are plentiful and less expensive. You can also save money by using more greenery and ribbon as filler in your bouquets.

I have also included a sample flower order form for you to review. Read over this typical contract and its terms. Ask your florist of choice for a copy of his or her form. Take it home and review it carefully. If you have questions or disagree with any of the terms, discuss them with your florist and make adjustments (*in writing*) on the contract so that you feel secure and pleased with the agreement. Remember, too, that both you *and* your florist should sign your agreement. This makes the terms of the agreement binding on *both* parties.

For your convenience, I have also included a floral schedule in this chapter. It can be removed, copied and given to your floral coordinator to ensure fast and accurate placement of all of your wedding flowers on your special day.

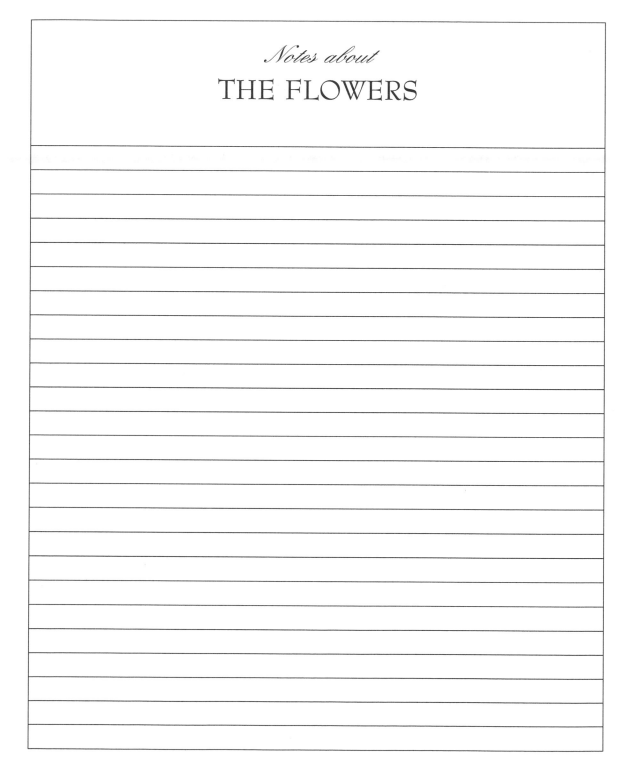

Notes about

THE FLOWERS

Flower Guideline
VENDOR INFORMATION

WHEN TO MAKE ARRANGEMENTS

Begin florist shopping no sooner than 7 months and no later than 3 months before the wedding day.

Visit at least 3 florists and keep notes.

WHERE TO FIND THE BEST

Friends and relatives can recommend florists.

Also consult your reception coordinator and your photographer.

Check local bridal shows and watch for floral arrangements you see at other parties or special occasions.

WHAT TO WATCH OUT FOR

- Always check to see if any of your attendants may be allergic to certain flowers.

WHAT IT WILL COST

No more than 15% of your total wedding budget should be spent on your flowers.

If you give a creative florist a specific budget and the amount and variety of flowers you want, he or she can realistically develop a "flower plan" for you.

Referring another customer can also save you a 10% discount.

A WEDDING CUSTOM OR TRADITION

In England, the bride carries a plastic horseshoe in her wedding bouquet for good luck. She also gives her female attendants a cutting of myrtle (symbolizing love) from her bouquet. According to custom, if the plant roots and blooms, they will marry soon.

*A
Wedding
Wi$e
Tip*

Always include your
favorite flower in your wedding bouquet.
It will bring you good luck.

**IMPORTANT
FACTS TO KNOW**

1. Nationally, florists agree that it is the bride's personality that is the most important factor in designing her wedding bouquet.
2. A bridal bouquet can be *any* color.
3. Traditionally, the groom's boutonniere matches one of the flowers in the bride's bouquet, and it is *different* from the groomsmen's.
4. Groomsmen's boutonnieres are generally white in color, but can also match the bridesmaids' dress color.
5. You can save money by using more greenery and ribbon as a filler in your wedding bouquets.
6. Carnations are the least expensive and most commonly used flower for wedding bouquets.
7. Florists can also preserve a bridal bouquet. Be sure to ask about this.
8. Silk flowers can be dyed to match *any* color. Today, silk reproductions are so lifelike that most people attempt to smell them. Plus, they never wilt, thus providing a lasting wedding keepsake.
9. A new aisle runner trend is the use of a 36-inch-wide bolt of white lace instead of the traditional white cotton.
10. Mothers and grandmothers can wear their corsages on the bodice, at the waist, on the wrist or attached to a handbag.
11. It is the groom who generally pays for the wedding flowers.
12. Ask your florist about a breakaway wedding bouquet. A concealed center (or a bottom tail, if yours is a cascade bouquet) is removable. You toss the breakaway corsage, and keep the rest of your bouquet.
13. As you walk down the aisle, your right arm is crossed over your escort's arm. Your left hand holds your bouquet—at your *side*. Don't hide your beautiful gown with an overwhelming floral bouquet.

Flower Guideline
SAMPLE FLORAL ORDER

Flowers for the Wedding

Name _____

Date _____ Time _____

Ceremony Site _____

Reception Site _____

THE BRIDE

Color/Style of Gown

Style of Bouquet

THE BRIDAL PARTY

Honor Attendant
Color/Style

Bridesmaids (#   )
Color/Style

Flower Girl (#   )
Color/Style

BOUTONNIERES

Groom

Best Man

Groomsmen (#   ) _____

Fathers _____ Grandfathers _____

Ring Bearer Others

CORSAGES

Bride's Mother _____

Groom's Mother _____

Grandmothers (#   ) _____

Others

(continued)

CEREMONY DECOR

Main Altar _____

Aisle Runner _____

Pew Decorations _____

Other _____

RECEPTION

Cake Table _____

Head Table _____

Buffet Table _____

Centerpieces _____

Other

Accepted By _____ Date _____ Subtotal _____

Accepted By _____ Date _____ Sales Tax _____

TOTAL _____

Read cancellation and refund policy (back side)   Deposit _____

If you do not agree with something, put a line through it.   Balance Due _____

(This means it will not apply to your wedding flower order.)

*Buyer*_____ *For Seller*_____

BE SURE they sign, too!

Flower Guideline
COST COMPARISONS

LOCATION	1	2	3
Florist's Name			
Address			
Contact Person			
Phone			
Hours Open			
Appointment Time			
PERSONAL FLOWERS			
Bride			
Throwaway			
Bridesmaids (#)			
Bride's Mother			
Groom's Mother			
Grandmothers (#)			
Godmothers			
Groom's Boutonniere			
Boutonnieres (#)			
CEREMONY FLOWERS			
Altar Flowers			
Candelabras, Candles			
Pew Deocrations			
Arch/Canopy			
Aisle Runner			
RECEPTION FLOWERS			
Head Table			
Buffet Table			
Centerpieces			
Cake Table			
Guestbook Stand			
Other			
Delivery/Setup			
Total Cost			
Deposit Required			
Balance Due When			
Cancellation Policy			

Flower Guideline
OUR FLORAL SCHEDULE

(This page can be removed and given to your floral coordinator.)

Florist's Name _____

ITEM	TYPE OF FLOWERS	# ENCLOSED
BOUQUETS		
Bride		
Toss Bouquet		
Maid of Honor		
Bridesmaids		
CORSAGES		
Mothers		
Grandmothers		
Aunts		
BOUTONNIERES		
Groom		
Best Man		
Ushers		
Fathers		
Grandfathers		
CEREMONY		
Arches		
Canopy		
Staircase		
Entrance Hall		
Altar		
Pews		
Aisle Carpet		
RECEPTION		
Head Table		
Cake Table		
Buffet Table		
Centerpieces		

Person responsible for handing out flowers _____
Person responsible for bridal bouquet preservation _____
Person responsible for cleanup after ceremony _____

PRE-WEDDING PARTY GUIDELINE

This chapter is all about *fun* and *excitement*. It describes various traditional pre-wedding parties that you will want to include as part of your wedding festivities.

The *bridal luncheon* can be held at a home, local restaurant or a hotel party room. I have included a special comparison page for your cost and record keeping. I have also added a party outline. It will help you to organize all of the details for this unique "ladies only" celebration.

For the *bachelor bash*, I have included a name roster. The best man will ask for the names of important people from the families who should be invited to this party. After you or your fiancé have filled in the blanks, simply remove the page and hand it to the best man.

Most important is the *rehearsal dinner*. Consider local restaurants or small hotel party rooms. Shop around, check menu costs and keep notes on the comparison page in this chapter. Review the chart that I have designed for your rehearsal dinner program. Remember—this party sets the pace for the entire wedding celebration. You will want to create an organized evening that is both fun and entertaining for all.

Notes about

PRE-WEDDING PARTIES

Pre-Wedding Party Guideline
FACTS AND INFORMATION

THE BRIDAL LUNCHEON

This "ladies only" party is attended by the bride, bridesmaids, mothers and grandmothers. It can be a brunch, an afternoon barbecue or a formal dinner party, at home or at a restaurant. It can even be a pajama party. A special "bride's cake" is usually served as the dessert. A thimble or wedding ring is baked into the cake. The person who gets the trinket in her piece of cake is said to be the next to marry. The bride may also give her attendants their gifts at this party.

❧

THE BACHELOR BASH

This traditional "last hurrah" party celebrates the end of the groom's bachelorhood, and is usually hosted by the best man. It can be a night on the town, a private "at home" beer party, an evening at the races or a sporting event followed by a meal at a restaurant. It is usually held a few days before the wedding, so that the groom and others can recover from the celebrating.

❧

THE WEDDING REHEARSAL

Your wedding rehearsal is the only "practice" that any person involved in your wedding ceremony will get to know what to do and when to do it. *All* participants must attend the rehearsal—including the little attendants. Copies of your ceremony program will provide the outline they should follow. An experienced officiant will rehearse the "entire" ceremony, allowing each person to go up to the podium to practice his or her lines. If it is possible, rehearse with music. One important tip: Don't over-rehearse children.

❧

THE REHEARSAL DINNER

This is the last pre-wedding party. It follows the rehearsal on the day before the wedding. This party, which can be *any* kind of party, is usually hosted by the groom's parents. However, close friends, godparents or relatives may also sponsor this celebration. Everyone who is participating in the wedding ceremony is invited to this party. It is also courteous to include any visiting out-of-town relatives. During the party, special toasts are made and attendants may be given their gifts.

❧

THE POST-WEDDING BRUNCH

This party is a late morning get-together held the day after the wedding. Usually the parents of either the bride or the groom host this party at their home. It usually includes a buffet or a continental breakfast. If the wedding couple is still in town, they are the guests of honor, and can open any wedding gifts, if they wish. This party serves as an excellent farewell celebration for all of the out-of-town relatives and friends.

❧

Pre-Wedding Party Guideline
COST COMPARISONS—Bridal Luncheon Sites

LOCATION	1	2	3
Party Site			
Address			
Contact Person			
Phone			
Dates Open			
# of Guests			
MENU CHOICE, COST			
#1			
#2			
#3			
Drinks (Average Cost)			
Gratuity			
Room Charge			
Entertainment			
Decorations Allowed			
Estimated Total			
Deposit Required			
Balance Due When			
Cancellation Policy			

Pre-Wedding Party Guideline
MY BRIDAL LUNCHEON OUTLINE

Date _____ Time _____ # Attending _____

Selected Site _____ Address _____

City _____ State _____ Zip _____ Phone _____

MENU _____ Special Dessert _____

_____ _____

Gifts/Favors _____

Decorations I Want _____

GUEST LIST FOR THE PARTY			
NAME	PHONE	NAME	PHONE

Pre-Wedding Party Guideline
THE BACHELOR BASH

(This page can be removed and given to the best man.)

Although women *never* attend this party, it is correct for the bride to know about it, and to help with its planning, if necessary. This could include food preparation and serving. It is also helpful to provide the best man with a list of the men in her family who should be invited.

BRIDE'S AND GROOM'S FAMILY AND FRIENDS FOR THE BACHELOR BASH			
NAME	PHONE	NAME	PHONE

Pre-Wedding Party Guideline
COST COMPARISONS—Rehearsal Dinner Sites

LOCATION	1	2	3
Party Site			
Address			
Contact Person			
Phone			
Dates Open			
# of Guests			
MENU CHOICE, COST			
#1			
#2			
#3			
Drinks (Average Cost)			
Gratuity			
Room Charge			
Entertainment			
Decorations Allowed			
Estimated Total			
Deposit Required			
Balance Due When			
Cancellation Policy			

Pre-Wedding Party Guideline
OUR REHEARSAL DINNER PROGRAM

Party Site _____

Address _____

Date _____ Time _____

Cocktails Before Dinner Toasts:	Given By:
A Toast to the Wedding Couple	Bride's Father, Brother
A Toast to the Bride	Mother of the Bride
A Toast to the Groom	Groom's Father, Best Man

Dinner Served Menu Selections:

_____

_____

_____

_____

_____

After Dinner Roasts, Toasts and Stories:	Given By:
A Toast to the Bride and her parents	Groom
A Toast to the Groom and his parents	Bride

_____

_____

_____

Special Entertainment/Presentations

_____

_____

_____

Appreciation—Distribution of Gifts

_____

_____

_____

TRANSPORTATION GUIDELINE

If you want to travel in style on your wedding day, the chauffeur-driven limousine is the most fashionable and truly deluxe mode of travel. The most traditional type of limousine used for a wedding is called a "stretch" vehicle. This means that you can order a Cadillac, Lincoln, Mercedes-Benz or Rolls-Royce equipped with all of the following: a surround-sound stereo system, one or two fully stocked service bars, a color television with a VCR, a moon roof and matchbooks with your names and wedding date engraved on them. All of this is neatly separated by a one-way glass divider between the driver and passengers. For an additional fee, some companies will even fill the vehicle with color-coordinated helium balloons.

The newest modes of wedding travel are limo-vans and old-fashioned yellow school buses (to accommodate the entire large bridal party). Other unique options include caravans of vintage cars, old fire engines, cycles built for two and, for superfast getaways, a helicopter.

Carefully review the costs that I have outlined in this chapter. As you shop around, make notes and keep them on the comparison page. When placing your order, be sure to *write out* all of the details of your arrangements, including all pickup point locations. Above all, watch out for any add-on gratuity fees or extra mileage charges. Be careful now, so you won't be sorry later.

Notes about

TRANSPORTATION

Transportation Guideline
VENDOR INFORMATION

WHEN TO MAKE ARRANGEMENTS

Reservations are necessary for all luxury rental vehicles.

Make reservations 2 months before the wedding date.

During prom time or holidays, plan 3 months in advance.

WHERE TO FIND THE BEST

Reputable limousine companies advertise in the yellow pages, often including photos of the vehicles they offer.

At local bridal shows limousines are sometimes displayed for your personal inspection.

WHAT TO WATCH OUT FOR

- Find out if the 15% gratuity (given to driver) can be automatically added to your total bill and paid at the time of pickup.
- Also check if you will be responsible for any service or travel fees based on the total miles put on the vehicle for your event.

WHAT IT WILL COST

Limousines are usually charged by hourly use. Expect to pay $50 to $200 per hour. A 3-hour minimum rental time is required. Many limousine companies now offer special "wedding packages" which include the vehicle and a set time period.

A 50% deposit is usually required. The balance is collected by the driver when the limousine *arrives* at the pickup point.

The driver *usually* collects a 15% gratuity at the *final* drop point.

A WEDDING CUSTOM OR TRADITION

The custom of tying shoes onto the back of the honeymoon getaway car dates back to the fifteenth century, when the father of the bride gave her shoes to her new husband to signify that she was now the groom's property.

A Wedding Wi$e Tip

If you don't use a limousine or specialty transportation, consider decorating a large car with bells, streamers and a "JUST MARRIED" sign to create a special wedding vehicle. These items are available at discount and party supply stores everywhere.

<table>
<tr><td>

IMPORTANT
FACTS
TO KNOW

</td><td>

1. Stretch limos are traditionally used for wedding transportation. They include a variety of luxuries: plush interiors, a bar, a telephone and a television with a VCR.
2. Today, Cadillacs, Lincolns, Mercedes, Rolls-Royce and streamlined vans are used for luxury transportation.
3. Vintage cars, sports cars, and full-size luxury cars can also be rented. Look in the yellow pages under "Automobile Rentals."
4. Horse-drawn carriages offer unique transportation and provide exciting photography subjects. They also may require a permit to use on city streets. Check with your local police station.

</td></tr>
</table>

Transportation Guideline
COST COMPARISONS—Luxury Vehicles

LOCATION	1	2	3
Company Name			
Address			
Contact Person			
Phone			
Dates Open			
Types of Vehicles			
Maximum Passengers			
Number Needed			
Rental Includes			
Rates Per Hour			
Special Wedding Packages			
Gratuity Fee			
Overtime Fees			
Estimated Total			
Deposit Required			
Balance Due When			
Cancellation Policy			

HONEYMOON GUIDELINE

National travel statistics show that 95 percent of all couples marrying this year will take some kind of honeymoon. It is important that you do your honeymoon homework in a timely manner because popular destinations are usually booked one year in advance, especially during their peak seasons.

While the number one choice today of honeymoon couples is the all-inclusive resort in a tropical setting, domestic honeymoons to places like Las Vegas, the Poconos or Florida cost 50 percent less.

Couples who marry on Friday can have a long-weekend honeymoon that also short-cuts costs. If you select a resort or recreational haven that is closer to home, you can drive and save, too. For best results, work with an experienced, reputable travel agent. Compare several destination choices and keep notes on the cost comparison page in this chapter. Also refer to the honeymoon outline in this chapter. You may wish to make a copy of this page to take with you for verification of your reservation.

Notes about

THE HONEYMOON

Honeymoon Guideline
VENDOR INFORMATION

WHEN TO MAKE ARRANGEMENTS

Reservations are necessary for all travel accommodations.

Begin investigating honeymoon destinations six months before the wedding.

Shop around and compare the differences in the vacation packages that are offered.

❧

WHERE TO FIND THE BEST

Find valuable information through travel sections of the local newspapers, newsstand magazines about travel, bridal magazine travel sections and personal visits to local travel agencies.

Also check your local library for their copy of the AT&T 800 Directory. You'll find all hotel chains, cruise companies and tourism and travel bureaus for every state in the country—plus all the calls are free.

❧

WHAT TO WATCH OUT FOR

• Be sure to get a written confirmation letter from your honeymoon hotel and *take it with you*. This letter specifies, in writing, your room rates, guaranteed dates of occupancy and any additional services that will be included in your rate.

WHAT IT WILL COST

The average honeymoon is a seven-day trip that costs approximately $2,500. This includes your airfare, hotel room, meals and beverages, taxes and gratuities and some spending money. Prices vary according to the seasons. During peak time, the highest rates are charged.

Save airfare costs by traveling on a weekday instead of a weekend. Evening flights are also less costly than those during daytime hours.

A Wedding Wi$e Tip

Be sure to check what your destination's normal weather conditions are for the time of year you are considering. Take your own camera and film or a handy single-use camera for your honeymoon candids. Prices for these items can be three times as expensive at the vacation site.

IMPORTANT
FACTS TO KNOW

1. *Always* work with a professional travel agent. Any person who is a member of the American Society of Travel Agents (ASTA) is a fully accredited travel professional. Look for one who specializes in honeymoons.
2. There is *no charge* to you to book your travel arrangements with a travel agent.
3. A honeymoon is any kind of private getaway. It can be one day or longer.
4. The most popular domestic honeymoon sites are Las Vegas, Florida, the Poconos and California.
5. Adventure honeymoons include rafting trips, camping and mountain cabin retreats.
6. The most popular honeymoon request is the all-inclusive resort usually located in the Caribbean. These resorts offer luxurious accommodations, food all day long, all drinks and most activities for *one price*. And there's no tipping allowed.
7. A cruise offers a floating city of food, fun, gambling and many planned activities. This kind of honeymoon is also all-inclusive!
8. If you travel outside of the United States, you may have to obtain a passport. They are available at local post offices and take 8–12 weeks to process.
9. Always use traveler's checks when traveling. Some traveler's checks charge a service fee at time of cashing—look for those that can be used at face value.
10. Make a list of all your luggage contents (for any loss claims).
11. Things to bring along:
    Your marriage license
    Your hotel confirmation letter
    Your driver's license
    Proof of age (birth certificate)
    Names and phone numbers of parents
    Name of your local drugstore
    List of credit card numbers

Honeymoon Guideline
COST COMPARISONS

LOCATION	1	2	3
Destination			
Passport Requirements			
Airfares/Other			
Resort/Hotel/Ship Name			
Contact Person			
Phone			
Rates			
Special Wedding Packages			
Meal Prices			
Beverage Prices			
Taxes/Gratuities			
Taxis, Shuttles/Costs			
Local Sightseeing			
Entertainment			
Sports Activities			
Spending Money			
Estimated Total			
Deposit Required			
Balance Due When			
Cancellation Policy			

Honeymoon Guideline
OUR HONEYMOON OUTLINE

Wedding Night Lodging _____

Address _____

Phone _____ Check-In _____

(Don't forget: The groom carries the bride over the threshold.)

Travel Agency	Agent

800#

Honeymoon Dates

TRAVEL RESERVATIONS

Date	Carrier	Departs	Arrives

RENTAL CAR RESERVATIONS

Agency

Phone	Rate/Confirmation #

Notes

HOTEL RESERVATIONS (Take your hotel confirmation letter with you.)

Honeymoon Site

Hotel Name

Address

Phone	Reservation Confirmation #
Arrival Date	Check-In
Departure Date	Check-In

Notes

LEGAL GUIDELINE

When you marry, most states in America require that you obtain a marriage license. This license is filed as a public record that registers your change in social status in the state in which you live. However, you are *not* legally married simply by obtaining a marriage license. It is *only* the act of marrying in front of witnesses, with all parties signing the license, that puts the contract of marrying into effect.

Once you are married, you and your husband will need to make your status and address changes known to the proper sources. Use my handy change guideline in this chapter. The page can be removed, copied and used by both of you.

For better convenience, I have also included a sample change form letter. The page can also be removed and copied. You simply fill in the change blanks and mail to all necessary parties.

Notes about

LEGAL REQUIREMENTS

Legal Guideline
STATUS AND ADDRESS CHANGES

(This page can be removed, copied and used by both bride and groom.)

Legal Policies and Documents	Name Change	Address Change	Account/Policy #	Telephone	Done
STATE RECORDS					
Driver's License					
Car Registration					
Social Security					
Property Titles					
Voter Registration					
IRS					
Post Office					
Passports					
MONEY MATTERS					
Credit Card					
Checking Accounts					
Savings Accounts					
IRA Accounts					
Stocks and Bonds					
Loans					
Wills/Trusts					
Leases					
INSURANCE					
Life Insurance					
Auto Insurance					
Property Insurance					
Medical Insurance					
PERSONAL					
Utilities					
Doctors					
Dentist					
Memberships					
Subscriptions					
School Records					
Stationery					
Other					

Legal Guideline
SAMPLE NAME CHANGE LETTER

(This page can be removed, copied and used for all necessary changes.)

Please Note: Brides can use this standard form letter, fill in the blanks and send it to all necessary agencies, with a copy of their marriage license. Some places, like the post office, require a visit with the copies. For department stores, simply cross out and print in the new name on the monthly statement or bill.

Today's Date _____

To Whom It May Concern,

This letter will serve as the formal notification of our marriage and request for a change of address. The account/policy number is _____
Under the name of _____

PRIOR DATA/RECORD

Husband's Name	Wife's Maiden Name
Previous Address	Previous Address
City State Zip	City State Zip
Phone	Phone

NEW INFORMATION

Husband's Full Name	Social Security Number
Wife's Full Name	Social Security Number

City   State   Zip   Phone

We were married on _____
(See attached copy of our marriage license.)

Please change name ☐   address and telephone ☐   add spouse's name ☐

Please send all necessary forms to complete this process. If there are any questions, please contact us at your earliest convenience.

Sincerely,

Mr. _____

Mrs. _____

$\mathscr{V}$ENDOR LIST AND RECORD OF DEPOSITS

$\mathbf{K}$eep all of your vendors, contact people and their telephone numbers at your fingertips with the following master vendor list. Next, the record of deposits will help you to keep accurate track of when and how much money you are spending, as you proceed to walk down the aisle.

MASTER VENDOR LIST

VENDOR	CONTACT	BEST TIME TO CALL	PHONE #
Jeweler			
Wedding Consultant			
Clergyman			
Bridal Gown Retailer			
Maid's Retailer			
Formal Wear Shop			
Reception Director			
Caterer			
Clergy			
Church Music Director			
Reception Entertainment Specialty Entertainment			
Invitations			
Photography			
Florist			
Baker			
Videographer			
Transportation Companies			
Travel Agent			
Beautician			
Balloon Decorator			

RECORD OF DEPOSIT

Date	Payment Made To	Amount of Deposit	Method of Payment	Balance Due	Date Due